Mike + Cathy,   Aug '04

Thanks for the taste of
"the Coast" - hope this
helps with
future
adventures.
Lynne
XO

PADDLING
THE
SUNSHINE
COAST

PADDLING
THE
SUNSHINE
COAST

Dorothy
&
Bodhi
Drope

Harbour
Publishing

Harbour Publishing • Box 219 • Madeira Park • BC • V0N 2H0

Cover design by Martin Nichols, Lionheart Graphics • Page design by David Lee Communications • All maps, illustrations and photographs by Dorothy and Bodhi Drope unless otherwise credited • Cover photograph by Bodhi Drope • Printed and bound in Canada.

Canadian Cataloguing in Publication Data

Drope, Dorothy 1937–
  Paddling the Sunshine Coast

  Includes index.
  ISBN 1-55017-164-X

  1. Sea kayaking—British Columbia—Sunshine Coast—Guidebooks. 2. Sunshine Coast (B.C.)—Guidebooks. I. Drope, Bodhi,
1931– II. Title.
GV788.5.D76 1997   797.1'224'0971131   C97-910124-7

Table of Contents

Acknowledgements

The authors wish to express special thanks to Andre Lapointe, always there and willing to share his paddling expertise. Other paddlers who have contributed to our skill development are Chris Gerow, Brian Henry, Don Jamieson, Dan Lewis and Marty Rosen.

To him who in the love of Nature
holds communion with her visible forms,
she speaks a various language.

—*William Cullen Bryant*

Introduction

While strolling the beach at English Bay in Vancouver one afternoon, I noticed a young man playing in the waves in a very small watercraft. As he came closer, I saw a sea kayak for the first time. This triggered an all-consuming desire to try it! I rented a kayak on Granville Island and out I went. I was in heaven! The ease with which this little craft moved through the water, the intimacy between me and the sea, the lovely day—all seduced me into a state of joy.

Cruising the seawall at Stanley Park, I eventually found myself heading into Burrard Inlet. Drifting along so easily, in my state of joyful intoxication, I was completely unaware that it is illegal to enter a commercial waterway such as this in a boat without a motor. Before long I caught sight of fast-moving water just ahead, which soon became rapids. Hey, this prairie girl did not understand lakes that suddenly became rivers. With much effort I got turned around, and then found myself struggling to paddle against a strong force that seemed bent on moving me backwards. Eventually I broke free. I had had my first encounter with a tidal current.

In spite of this harrowing experience, I was hooked and could barely wait to share my story with Bodhi.

—*Dorothy*

It was Dorothy's raving that prompted me to try sea kayaking. I must admit the very idea filled me with fear due to a near drowning I had in my younger years. I simply could not imagine anyone in their right mind venturing off shore in such a small craft. Somewhere out at sea, that feeling eventually dissolved.

We were in our middle years when we had these first experiences and now, many years and many miles later, kayaking has become a major part of our lives, providing us with exciting adventures along the magnificent coast of BC. An unexpected and most gratifying benefit is realizing just how physically fit it keeps us. The fresh air, the hours we spend in a natural environment and the full upper body workouts have had a positive effect on both of us.

Always keen readers, we have bought and enjoyed many books on kayaking on the Pacific coast. But it became obvious that the majority of these books were written for "young jocks." We did not fit into this mold. Our love of kayaking came from the opportunity to be intimate with the marine environment, poking along in the intertidal zone and hanging out to allow the wildlife to come to us.

Kayaking at Jedediah Island

We also noted that our own home area, the Sunshine Coast from Howe Sound to Desolation Sound, had not been chronicled in a paddling guidebook as yet. This prime paddling country offers everything the paddler could possibly ask for to enjoy the sport to the fullest—magnificent panoramic views, fascinating marine gardens, lots of wildlife, plenty of marine parks and campgrounds as well as comfortable accommodation and good restaurants for the "jock-less" types.

With all this firmly in mind, we began to document our trips—Dorothy scrambling for pen and pad to capture a fleeting monumental moment and me with camera and drawing instruments close on her stern. Every inch of this coastline has inspired our artistic bent and seduced our poetic natures, while occasionally challenging the "jock" deep within.
—*Bodhi*

The novice should realize the Sunshine Coast will always offer a satisfying outing because of the many different trips available in such a compact area. For example, if a strong westerly is blowing on the Strait of Georgia, look to the Sechelt Inlet or explore Gibsons Harbour.

If you want to take photographs from a kayak, you have to have your camera set up and ready to go. Bodhi carries his camera and telephoto lens between his chest and life jacket, and stores the other lenses in a hard case dry bag between his legs. This permits a quick grab, aim and shoot for the instantaneous response. Your choice of shots is unlimited—mountain views with snow and all, flocks of seabirds, darting kingfishers, oystercatchers foraging the shoreline with their long red bills, eagles plunging down and striking the sea, then slowly rising carrying large flapping fish.

Before you embark on your paddling trips on the Sunshine Coast, we recommend that you read the information on weather, tides, safety equipment and special cautions. We have included some basic wisdom that will help you improve your knowledge and skills as a paddler.

We also recommend you honestly assess your strengths and weaknesses when you plan your trip, and that you don't take on more than you are ready for. Common sense cannot be taught, rented or purchased but it remains the fundamental factor in your safety and enjoyment of the sport of paddling.

We have greatly enjoyed gathering all the information in this book and exploring the various trips the Sunshine Coast has to offer. Our wish is that you too will have as much fun. Kayaking offers something for every age and level of fitness. Get out there and reap the physical and spiritual benefits for yourself.

See you on the water!   —*Dorothy and Bodhi*

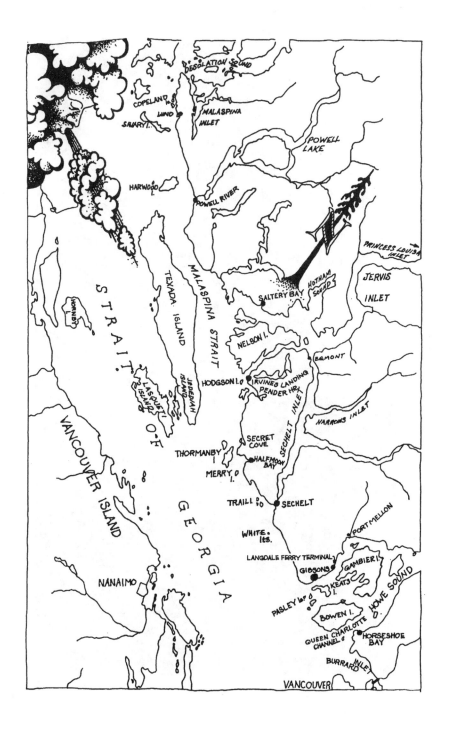

The Sunshine Coast

The stretch of coastline from Howe Sound in the south to Desolation Sound in the north along the east side of the Strait of Georgia bears the name the Sunshine Coast. The name was coined by Harry Roberts, celebrated scion of the first family of Roberts Creek. He painted "The Sunshine Belt" in large letters on his shed in hopes of attracting the tourist trade. This later evolved into the Sunshine Coast. The name has been creeping up the coast since that beginning to include first the Egmont–Jervis Inlet area and more recently the Powell River district and Desolation Sound.

The coast has long been a refuge for writers, painters and artists of every ilk as well as home to the fishers and loggers drawn to the wealth of the natural environment. A rich variety of rugged individualists fleeing the constraints of the city have found peace and freedom in the relative isolation. These days, the Sunshine Coast has also become a haven for retired people.

Natives of the Coast

The Coast Salish peoples have shared the bounty of the Sunshine Coast since time began. The Squamish tribe of Howe Sound, the Sechelts of the Sechelt Peninsula and the Sliammon people of Powell River lived a life of relative peace and plenty along these shores. The abundance of food combined with the benign climate and traditions of government featuring respect for human life and individual freedom created an enviable lifestyle.

Before the impact of European settlement, there were about eighty villages in the area with major settlements of the Hunaechin subgroup at the head of Jervis Inlet, the Tsonai in Deserted Bay, the Tuwanek at the head of Narrows Inlet and in Porpoise Bay, and the Skaiakos in Garden Bay and on the Thormanbys. Large numbers would congregate for the winter in the Pender Harbour area.

They lived in single pitch plank longhouses with house fronts, ridgepoles and gables decorated with anthropomorphic figures of sea lions, seals, orca whales and the like. The Sechelts were particularly well known for twilled mountain goat wool blankets woven on roller looms.

The European invasion brought swift and devastating changes to aboriginal groups, including unfamiliar diseases and deliberate acts of cultural genocide. The Natives' work of reclaiming their proud traditions and control of their traditional lands continues. The Sechelts are well known and respected as the first Native group in Canada to achieve self-government, through the federal Sechelt Indian Self-Government Act of 1986. This act was modeled on municipal governments with additional powers in several areas. A year later the provincial government ratified the arrangement. This model has been challenged by many aboriginal groups in the country, but the Sechelts have apparently prospered under it. They are developing many enterprises on their lands that benefit their people and everyone in the community.

Weather

Weather, that very Canadian preoccupation, takes on new significance when you take up sea kayaking. Where a quick glance at the sky was once sufficient to tell you to take your umbrella, now you need a careful study that can affect your comfort and safety. Paddling is a considerable inducement to learn. Mankind has been watching the weather since time immemorial and attempting to predict the behaviour of these forces. Masses of weather lore have accumulated over the ages, but it remains difficult to predict weather reliably.

For the kayaker, wind is of the most concern because it

The minds of men do in the weather share,
Dark or serene as the day's foul or fair.

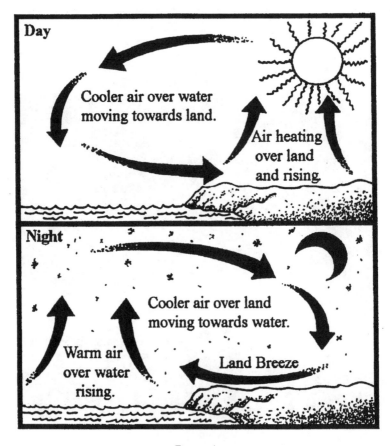

Day

Cooler air over water moving towards land.

Air heating over land and rising.

Night

Cooler air over land moving towards water.

Warm air over water rising.

Land Breeze

Figure A

produces waves and increases the work of paddling. As the front approaches, the wind increases, with the strongest winds just ahead of the front. Forecasting wind is difficult, as winds are produced by local topography, relative temperature of land and sea and weather systems. The topography of coastal BC, with its mountains, valleys, long inlets and peninsulas, produces local weather which affects the kayaker just as much as the larger weather systems. In fact, the paddler is much more likely

Red sky in morning, sailor take warning.
Red sky at night, sailor's delight.

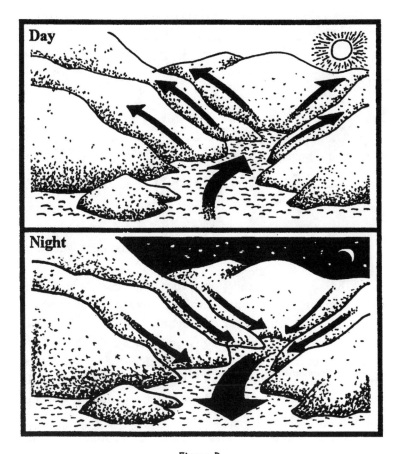

Figure B

to get caught in unexpected conditions generated by local topography than the big front that is forecasted and therefore expected.

The diurnal, or daily, winds result when the sun heats the earth more quickly than the water. Air flows from cool to warm and the wind blows on shore (Figure A). At night it blows off shore as the water cools more slowly than the land. These winds start in mid-morning, subside in late afternoon and rise again

Curls that kink and cords that bind:
Signs of rain and heavy winds.

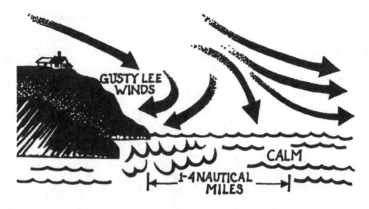

Figure C

after sunset. They are strongest on hot, sunny days when the prevailing winds are light.

Winds in valleys and along mountain slopes behave in a similar manner in response to the warming and cooling of sea and land (Figure B). During the day, the sides of valleys warm more rapidly than the bottoms and the winds—known as anabatic winds—flow up the slopes. At night the reverse occurs and the katabatic wind flows down the slopes. In the Sechelt Inlet, a deep valley flooded with sea water, you find these winds on most days of summer.

Outflow winds are a feature of winter weather along the coast. Cold Arctic air is pushed out toward the sea by the much higher pressure over the interior. It flows off the mountains like water pouring from a bucket, its force intensified by the funnelling effect. These winds, common in inlets or along coastlines adjacent to a valley, can fall on you like a hammer. The Squamish winds of Howe Sound are a local example.

The lee effects occur when winds blow against steep cliffs or offshore over rough terrain onto the water (Figure C). The resulting turbulence produces gusty winds and confused seas.

When the dew is on the grass,
Rain will never come to pass.

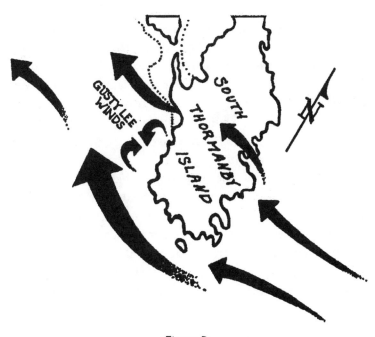

Figure D

Wind passing over land is slowed down more by friction than is wind passing over water. In some cases the coastal wind will veer toward the open water, but it may also curl toward the lee of a headland or an island, producing corner winds (Figure D) that are stronger than the prevailing winds. The paddler will notice these effects on headlands such as the south tip of Thormanby Island.

When you compress a hose, the force of the stream of water becomes much stronger. Similarly, when wind is squeezed through a narrow channel or gap—between two islands, for instance—its force is augmented considerably. Welcome Pass and Sabine Channel are local examples of this funnelling effect.

For long trips, we advise the paddler to consult all the numerous sources for information about weather and wind

Seaweed dry, sunny sky;
Seaweed wet, rain you'll get.

frequency in the trip area. Before setting out, listen to the radio for weather reports, call the closest Coast Guard station for the current marine weather report and observe local conditions carefully. It is advisable to carry a marine radio with you if you are on the water for more than a day or two. Always be prepared to change your plans to suit the weather, as it will not change to suit you. On Canada's Pacific coast, June to August is a time of mild, dry weather with long stretches of halcyon days where paddling is relatively safe and comfortable. Paddling in the off-season months can provide wonderful days of seclusion and quiet. Winter weather is changeable, so exercise more caution. Only deepest winter, from November to March, is unsuitable for kayak touring, but even that season will give you many nice days for short trips. We have paddled by mountain slopes covered in snow, watching the flocks of seabirds that winter in the protected inlets of the coast.

Weather Information for the Mariner:

Free recordings:
Vancouver (604) 666-3655 or 664-9010
Victoria (250) 656-2714 or 656-7515
Nanaimo (250) 245-8899
Sechelt (604) 885-0852 ext. 1144 (weather) / 1145 (marine weather)
When on shore talk directly to a weather forecaster (Weather One-On-One): 1-900-565-5555 (costs $1.95 per minute, 2-minute minimum); when offshore, or onshore, talk directly to a marine forecaster (WeatherCall—costs $5.00 first 3 minutes, then $1.95 per minute after). To register call (604) 664-9032 or fax (604) 664-9081

Weather on the Internet: www.weatheroffice.com

> *Rain long foretold, long last;*
> *Short notice, soon will past.*

Safety on the Water

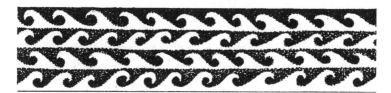

Each spring a small booklet with the tide tables for the year appears in local shops. This booklet tells you the tidal movements for each day of the year based on Point Atkinson in West Vancouver. It also tells you how to predict tides in areas where the local topography affects the tides greatly, such as the Sechelt Inlet.

If you can avoid paddling against the tidal flow or even use that flow to carry you forward, your trip will be easier and faster. We have taken trips where we went out with the ebb and returned with the flow. Many a paddler has whipped up an inlet with wind and tide at his back and then, to his dismay, found himself facing these forces on the return trip.

When wind blows against the direction of the tide, it affects the configuration of the waves. They become closer together and steeper, often causing them to break. This can have a considerable effect on kayakers in narrow passes where both tide and wind are already intensified by channelling and funnelling effects. Welcome Pass between Thormanby Island and the mainland is a notable local example.

Many a newcomer to the ocean environment learns the hard way about the behaviour of tides. This is not necessary. When establishing your campsite, identify the high tide line (that is, the highest high) before setting camp and storing your kayak for the night. Look for the highest line of debris along the beach.

The low high line will be washed away by the higher tide line. Be sure you know where you are in the cycle before setting up (see below).

Special Cautions for Kayakers

We have no desire to inhibit your sense of adventure, but we do wish to instill a healthy respect for the forces of nature with which you will contend on the Sunshine Coast. Of course, part of the appeal of kayaking is the risks and challenges imposed by these forces. But ideally, kayakers will emerge from all encounters stronger and more confident, feeling that their skills, knowledge and judgement have been sharpened. We hope you will try to learn all you can by every means available, and we offer a few tips on enjoying a challenging paddle without putting yourself in danger.

Most open water crossings described in the trips in this

The perfect spot

If you want to camp on the shore, remember the tides.

6 hours later

volume are 1.6 km (1 mile) or less. These crossings can be accomplished in 30 to 40 minutes even in less-than-perfect conditions. The paddler who stays alert and reacts quickly to changes will be ahead of the game. Conditions change most rapidly in winter as a rule. Longer crossings elevate the risk factors and require keener judgement.

When you undertake to do open water crossings and longer trips, we strongly recommend that you acquire the skills involved in self rescues and assisted rescues, and practise these on a regular basis.

Looking at the map of the area, find the Skookumchuck Narrows at the top of the Sechelt Inlet. Notice the topography, a narrow little river through which the full tidal exchange of that large inland sea must pass. This fact alone will tell you that the tidal currents here are going to be pretty awesome, and so it is. The rapids are impressive indeed. This is your first lesson in interpreting a map—that configuration means problems. Look at Malibu Rapids at the mouth of Princess Louisa Inlet for a similar situation. These spots become benign with the slack tide, so with local knowledge and a good understanding of the tide, you can pass easily through these particular waters.

Now look at Welcome Pass, between the mainland and South Thormanby Island. Again note the configuration is a narrow pass which is aligned with the direction of the prevailing winds, bordered by steep cliffs on either side which funnel and strengthen the winds and tidal currents. This is an area to approach cautiously on the ebb tide when the prevailing southeasterly blows.

The Squamish, an outflow wind, occurs in Howe Sound. A mass of cold air develops over the snow-covered mountains. Some event, such as a local wind gust, then destabilizes the mass and it pours down the mountains to the sea. Like water through a siphon, it pulls itself along the path of least resistance—a long, mountain-lined fjord. The wind flows in a jet out to sea through Barfleur Passage, which you must cross to visit the Pasley Islands. When the snowcap melts in summer, these winds are less frequent.

The prevailing southeast winds in the Strait of Georgia are often strongest on the Sunshine Coast where the long fetch, or length of the blow, increases the wave height.

Fog and rain occurring in the winter months in the Strait of Georgia decrease visibility on the water. Extra vigilance is necessary when paddling in areas of high marine traffic, such as Howe Sound, where you must rely on your ears and your compass to avoid collision. Most paddling on the Sunshine Coast is done close to the land, making it unnecessary to use a compass. Courses are set using bearings on landmarks, such as islands or ridges. On the other hand, we find navigation skills interesting to learn and fun to practise.

Even in the best of weather, a kayak is not easy to see from the bridge of a large boat. The highest risk of collision occurs in clear weather when complacency can relax caution. There are fewer incidents of collision or near collision when visibility is reduced.

Most risks are best avoided by paying attention to weather forecasts before you embark on your trip and being constantly aware of the ever-changing conditions around you. If you are always ready to simply wait out adverse conditions, you will be much safer. This means taking with you on every trip some basic survival gear—warm clothes, food, matches, flares and protection from rain.

Learn to read the sky and sea, focussing on your total environment at frequent intervals to assess the conditions as they change around you. This is part of the appeal of kayaking—continually bringing yourself into the here and now.

Tide, What Tide?

That loathsome sound of a telephone in the early morning hours ruined my sleep!

"Is this Bodhi?"

I respond with an incoherent mumble.

"I'm calling on behalf of Ed. He and his wife took one of your double kayaks on an overnight up the Sechelt Inlet."

He's definitely got my attention now. "Oh yes, that's right. Anything wrong?"

"Well, ah, yes. Ed and Mildred are presently up the creek without a paddle. Let me rephrase that—they're up the inlet without a kayak!"

"They're *what?*"

"Ed lost the boat sometime during the night. When they arose this morning they couldn't find the kayak. It's gone!" He described how Ed had carefully packed all their food, clothing and gear in the boat, completely forgetting about the high tide that would eventually hit the beach.

Fortunately, Ed remembered that he had his cellular phone in the tent. He called this chap down in Porpoise Bay, who agreed to rescue them with his outboard.

As soon as he hung up, we notified the police in case the double was located and they assumed a drowning had occurred. Later that day we heard from an Egmont fisherman. Taking his fishing boat home through the notorious Skookumchuck, he noticed a large shape going round and round in a bay close to the rapids. When he got close enough, he realized it was a kayak caught and held in a back eddy. The maverick double had been corralled.

As they climbed into their truck to drive back to Edmonton, the tension between the retired farmer and his wife could be cut with a knife. Mildred had not wanted to go kayaking. She was extremely nervous of water, wild animals, sleeping in a tent and especially of putting her life at risk in such a tiny boat. Ed had *convinced her they would have fun and be safe. I'll bet they are now getting lots of laughs telling the story back in Alberta.*

Dorothy and I smiled as they drove away, having learned a tough lesson on the rise and fall of ocean tides.

The Rules of the Road

You will be sharing a large part of your paddling environment with others of your kind—a particular hazard, we think you will agree.

The "Rules of the Road," or just "The Rules," are all the laws that dictate the behaviour of all vessels on all waters. You may not be able to learn everything about this incredibly complex subject, but you do need to learn the basics. The channels of Howe Sound and the coast of Georgia Strait are used extensively by commercial traffic.

Shipping lanes are marked with dotted lines on the maps. Cross these at right angles after carefully choosing the time. When crossing ferry routes, it is imperative that you know the ferry schedule before setting out. You have an interval of one hour between ferries to make your crossing.

Right-of-way is an extremely important rule of the road. Regulation number 1 is: "If he is bigger than you, he has the right-of-way." There are two reasons for this: the larger vessel is harder to manoeuvre, and the operators of the larger vessel may not be able to see you in your smaller vessel, even if they were able to avoid you. You should never be closer than 400 m (¼ mile) to the side or 800 m (½ mile) to the front of a larger ship. It may appear to be moving slowly, but in reality it is travelling much faster than you realize. Don't be tempted to sprint across the bow of one of these boats—this can result in heavy fines even if you survive the experience. Ignorance of the rules is no defence.

The only time you have the so-called right-of-way is when a vessel is overtaking you. Here your obligation is to maintain your course while he adjusts his course to avoid you. Use common sense in the case of the really big guys.

That said, all vessels approaching you must be aware of your limitations and make obvious moves to avoid collision. The same rule applies to you—it is up to you to be aware of the difficulty, for instance, of turning a tug, stopping a ferry or moving a tanker out of a shipping lane, and to take evasive action yourself. You must constantly assess the risk of collision with another vessel by every means at hand. A vessel coming straight for you will alter course to the starboard (right) and you should do the same. The "angle of the bow method" is a good way of determining if another vessel is on a collision course. Figure E (page 30) illustrates this simple technique. Try it each time you are approaching another boat until it becomes second nature to you. Remember to keep the same heading when you assess this angle.

The paddler should always bear in mind that it is very hard to see a kayak on the water, especially in choppy seas. We once paddled in a marathon across the Strait of Georgia in 3- to 4-foot seas. When we developed trouble with the rudder, we had to pull our kayak aboard the escort boat to make repairs. We immediately went to the front to see where our paddling partner was, and he was out of sight! From the bow of our 9-m (30-foot) escort boat he had vanished in minutes. Skippers of large vessels often voice their concerns about kayakers' lack of seamanship and the extreme difficulty of spotting their boats on the water.

Cold Water Survival

When you or a member of your party dumps and someone is in the water, hypothermia is the concern. In winter waters, that concern is intensified.

Hypothermia is the lowering of deep body temperature resulting in shock and depression of vital body functions. Symptoms of dysfunction will begin after 10 to 15 minutes in water

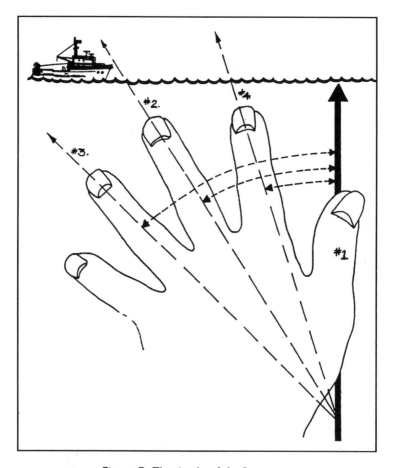

Figure E: The Angle of the Bow
Depending from which direction the ship is approaching:
1. Place the proper hand palm down on deck.
   Line your thumb up with the centre line of kayak.
   Spread fingers out.
2. Look down your fingers and line one finger up with the ship's bow.
   Check again.
3. If angle increases, the ship will pass behind.
4. If angle decreases, the ship will pass in front.
5. If the angle neither increases nor decreases, you are on a
   collision course.

at 10°C (50°F) and survival for the average adult is about 2½ to 3 hours in the water.

If you capsize in winter waters, your most critical tasks are to get help and to get out of the water as quickly as possible. As soon as trouble develops, fire off your first flare to attract attention to your plight. Do not wait to see whether you can correct the situation yourself, as delay is dangerous.

Begin your rescue with a view to getting the person into the kayak, pumping the water out and securing him in the kayak with the spray skirt. Remember that a person who has been in cold water will be shocked, which can contribute to another upset. Stay close by and do not remove the paddle float until you are positive that the person will remain upright. You may need to tow him to shore with the paddle float in place.

Once ashore, the priority is to warm the person up gradually. Do not offer alcohol, tea or coffee. Remove wet clothing only if replacements are available, or if he can be wrapped in blankets or moved indoors. Do not rub his limbs or handle him roughly. If he is uninjured and fully conscious, exercise (eg. walking, swinging arms) will aid in rewarming. It is best to put him in a sleeping bag with another warm person. Concentrate on warming the core of the body rather than the extremities. Continue to summon help with your flares.

Safety Tips and Equipment

If you are expecting to paddle in Canadian waters, you should know that regulations require you to meet minimum standards. Canadian regulations approve personal flotation devices (PFDs) only in orange, yellow and red, while in the US no such restrictions apply.

A jacket with lots of pockets on the front will always be useful for carrying safety gear such as flares, as well as a snack, your binoculars and the variety of other little gizmos that increase your comfort and enjoyment while paddling.

For us a pair of good binoculars is a necessity. Enjoying

wildlife is a major focus of our trips and binoculars increase that pleasure immeasurably. Tucked in a pocket of your PFD or down the front of your spray skirt, they are always at hand so you don't miss those once-in-a-lifetime encounters. Binoculars also allow you to review the terrain of a beach before you paddle in to prepare for your landing, which makes them invaluable for safety as well as convenience.

Regardless of the type of boat you have, it must be outfitted with adequate flotation fore and aft. Safety equipment in good operating order, easily accessible and of the type approved by the Canadian Department of Transport must be included.

You should have easy access to drinking water at all times, summer or winter, and develop the habit of sipping constantly. Dehydration increases fatigue and exacerbates the effects of hypothermia in the event of a spill.

Minimum safety equipment:
Water
Spray skirt
Paddle
Spare paddle (at least one per party)
Pump
Paddle float
Whistle or other sound signalling device
Life jacket or personal flotation device
Tow line (minimum 7.5 m/25 feet)

Items that should be with you at all times:
Waterproof matches and tinder (a bit of tarpaper or rubber is good)
Rain gear and light but warm clothes
Change of clothing and a sleeping bag in a waterproof bag (in winter)
Flares (at least 3), stored in an easily available spot, like the front pocket of your PFD or spray skirt
First aid kit

Basic repair kit for mending cables and cracks in fibre-
glass (duct tape)
Knife (serrated blade is recommended)
Compass and chart
Weather radio (marine radio if possible)
Plenty of rope, especially if you are camping
Binoculars, waterproof if possible, for scoping out landing
sites and enjoying wildlife watching

Over the years we have taken a variety of courses in kayaking
skills, and we recommend this to all who take up the sport. Not
only do the courses give you all the up-to-date safety tips, they
keep you keenly interested in the sport by encouraging you to
explore it more deeply.

The best defence against disaster is reliable equipment, the
knowledge to make informed choices and good kayaking skills.
Acquiring all this is part of the fun of the sport.

Wildlife Etiquette

In the US, the law states that boaters may not get closer than
110 yards (100 m) to any wildlife. Fines are levied when this
law is ignored. Canada has no laws at this time, but we
recommend the same behaviour. Experience has shown us that
animals remain calm and undisturbed if we keep this distance
away from them.

A number of areas on the coast are designated as bird or wildlife sanctuaries: Christie Islet and Pam Rock just southeast of Anvil Island in Howe Sound, the White Islets off the coast at Davis Bay, and Franklin Islet immediately west of Merry Island at the mouth of Halfmoon Bay. Do not set foot on these bits of land. In the spring, when birds are brooding or raising young, they are particularly vulnerable to disturbance. A human visit can cause birds to panic and abandon their eggs, which exposes the eggs to predators and causes damage from cooling.

Similarly, the health of seals and sea lions can be compromised when people get too close. In our experience, they frequently show great curiosity about paddlers and follow us closely, popping up nearby to check us out. But they should never be startled while resting on their haulouts. They need their time out of the water to reoxygenate their blood in preparation for the next session of diving for food. When this rest is interrupted, their health is compromised, and pups can be injured in a stampede to the water.

Be aware that both birds and sea mammals are much more accustomed to the presence of motor boats than the little kayak. We recommend a pair of binoculars as a necessary part of your equipment.

Bears are a fact of life for anyone who ventures into the outdoors, including the paddler. The fear of bears is disproportionate to the actual threat—in the last 80 years or so, there have been about 80 deaths in all of North America—but like all wild animals, bears are potentially dangerous and should be treated with respect.

Most bear attacks are precipitated by a perceived threat to cubs, food supply or territory. The most dangerous bears are those that have come to associate humans with food. This means that the care you take with your food is ensuring not only your own safety but the safety of those who follow you. Always leave your campsite clean and pack your garbage out with you. Store food in airtight containers suspended in trees at least 3.5

Bear on the beach in Hotham Sound.

m (12 feet) off the ground and away from your campsite. This means you have to take enough rope with you to do the tying!

Do not consider your kayak an airtight container. We have seen a kayak badly mauled by a bear trying to get at the food in it. The only exception to this rule is when you anchor your kayak out in the water.

Never put food in your tent, as the smell lingers even after the food is gone, and you won't be thrilled to have a bear sniffing around your tent while you are sleeping. If you clean fish, dispose of the guts well out in the water.

Generally bears will avoid you if they know you are there. A surprise encounter causes fear and anxiety in both bear and human. Making noise—talking, laughing, banging rocks together—helps to let the bear know you are in the area, and as long as it doesn't see you as a source of food, it will beat a hasty retreat.

We like to camp on islands whenever possible as this

minimizes problems with bears and other critters. On shore, don't set up right beside a stream. Other animals also need fresh water and may visit the site you have chosen.

If you do come face to face with a bear, do not turn and run, as this may trigger its predator response. Back away slowly, talking quietly and waving your arms in a nonthreatening way.

"I used to believe
my teachers
three
until I heard
a silent
tree.
Now
I know
teachers be,
rocks,
waves, trees
and bumble bees."

Low-Impact Camping

Garbage and Human Waste

Just a few words about protocol in the woods. Sites close to large cities are particularly vulnerable to negative impacts from human use. The fresh water quality is a case in point. Be aware that the sea has the greatest capacity for cleansing fecal bacteria from the environment. Use cat holes or turned-over rocks below the high tide line, rather than the woods. The topsoil at the seashore is too thin to cope with any amount of human waste.

If you must use cat holes in the woods, be sure you are not close to any lakes, streams or other fresh water sources. Burn toilet paper or pack it out.

Do not eat shellfish or harvest any other food on any beach that is routinely used for camping.

Potable Water

Many campsites are located near streams flowing off a mountainside. This water is probably suitable for drinking in winter when the weather is colder and the volume of water is high. However, even in winter there is always the risk of giardiasis, or beaver fever, so we recommend that you take water with you or disinfect it before use by boiling it or using chemical treatment. By the way, the water you use to brush your teeth can infect you.

Campfires

Everyone loves a campfire, but extensive use of camping areas can seriously deplete the available wood. Cutting living trees or shrubs will soon destroy the natural beauty of a site.

If you do build a campfire, it is best to put it on the beach below the high tide line so the incoming water will cleanse the site, leaving it pristine for the next visitor. Alternatively, use a campfire site that was used before, to keep the marks of our passing to a minimum.

Put that fire out when you are finished! You are using lands that are particularly vulnerable to fire, especially in warmer weather.

Clean up the campsite when you leave. Carry all garbage out with you. If you use unofficial campsites, it is a nice touch to leave the site looking like nobody has been there. This means obliterating fire sites by turning over blackened rocks, covering stained sand and dispersing firewood.

Fire restrictions are in effect in most areas during the summer months, so you must take a camp stove with you.

The Trips

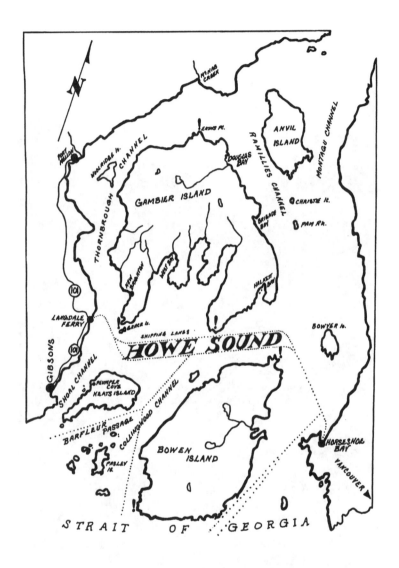

Howe Sound

Howe Sound, stretching from West Vancouver to Gibsons to Squamish, offers miles of protected waterways bound by majestic mountains rising straight out of the sea. Clusters of islands both large and small dot this seascape.

The largest of the islands is Gambier Island, which dominates the northeastern part of the Sound. While the south side of Gambier is deeply indented by a series of bays, the northern aspects are steeper with a few small bays to invite explorers.

Anvil Island, northeast of Gambier, rises steeply from the sea on all sides. It is believed to have been a sacred spot for the coastal Indians. Neither its history nor its geography encourages people to land on its shores, although there is a small beach on the east bank.

Just to the south of Anvil, tiny Christie Islet and Pam Rock provide ideal habitat for seals and a multitude of sea birds. These snippets of land are wildlife sanctuaries.

Bowen Island, also a very large island, guards the entrance to the Sound. Here we find a substantial and growing human population which dominates its shores except on the southern face.

The southern portion of Howe Sound is a bustle of activity,

with ferries plying the waters from Horseshoe Bay to Langdale and Nanaimo and countless commercial and recreational vessels going about their business.

In the northern reaches, the feeling of wilderness prevails. This is picturesque country, with craggy coastline, lush rain forest and streams—quiet in summer, full and turbulent in winter—coursing down the mountains to pour into the Sound. These waterways are home to a wide variety of wildlife, and the kayaker is in a unique position to see into their world.

From the Langdale ferry terminal to Lower Gibsons, the winding road follows the coastline, passing by homes and cottages in one of the fastest growing areas of BC. The place names here, such as Hopkins Landing and Granthams Landing, reflect a time when boats provided the only access to the coast. Today the area has grown to the point where individual "landings" blend into one another; the development is quite seamless and functions as one community.

The town of Gibsons sits at the southwest corner of the Sound just before it breaks out into the open water of the Strait

Howe Sound   Keith Thirkell photo

of Georgia. Tucked behind Steep Bluff at the mouth of Shoal Channel, the harbour is enclosed in the rocky arms of a man-made breakwater. Here you find the public wharf that is home to the local fishing fleet, and in the right season, you can buy fresh seafood off the boats. Wandering the floats gives you a taste of the fishing way of life.

The lower village is the oldest part of town and retains much of the charm of its fishing and logging past. Shops and restaurants serve visitors and locals alike. Molly's Reach, made famous by the popular CBC-TV show *The Beachcombers*, still guards the entrance to the public wharf. The walkway along the foreshore is perfect for a most enjoyable tour of the waterfront.

Looking across the channel you can see Keats Island with Plumper Cove Provincial Park on its northwest corner. This cove was named by Captain Richards, RN. He commanded the Royal Navy Survey Ship HMS *Plumper*, which surveyed the coast from November 1857 to January 1861. The park has sanitary facilities, water, picnic tables and campsites. The Shelter Islets protect the entrance to the cove, and farther southwest you can see the Keats Island public wharf and ferry landing, the focus of community life on the island.

On the east side of Keats Island, facing Bowen Island, lies Eastbourne. Another public wharf gives you access to this small settlement, where summer cottages built in the 1920s and 1930s are slowly giving way to modern homes for year-round residents. Rudimentary roads wind through the community and connect to the ferry landing across the island. For a pleasant walk in a woodsy, rural environment, give this a try.

The Pasley Islands appear to the south, clustered together between Keats and Bowen islands. Bound by Barfleur Passage to the north, Collingwood Channel to the east and the Strait of Georgia to the south, this group consists of five islands and a number of small islets. Pasley Island itself is by far the largest of these.

GETTING THERE

If you are driving from downtown Vancouver, proceed west on Georgia Street, cross the Lions Gate Bridge and drive on to the Upper Levels Highway (Highway 1 West). Follow the signs for the Horseshoe Bay ferry terminal and join the line for the Langdale ferry.

You can also take a bus to Horseshoe Bay, walk on the ferry, then board a local bus at the Langdale terminal and take it to Gibsons. In fact, you can take an early ferry from Horseshoe Bay, bus to Gibsons, rent a kayak, paddle for the day and return to Vancouver by early evening.

Or you can cycle to the ferry and then to Gibsons—a pleasant warm-up for the day's paddle.

Whether you're driving your car, taking the bus or cycling, the ferry trip from Horseshoe Bay to Langdale is a beautiful 40-minute trip through the splendour of Howe Sound. After you disembark at the Langdale terminal, turn left and follow the lower road to Gibsons.

GAMBIER ISLAND

WOOLRIDGE ISLAND AND EKINS POINT

GETTING THERE

From the Langdale ferry terminal, turn right at the first intersection (there is no launching spot at the terminal). If you are starting from Gibsons, follow the Port Mellon highway past the ferry terminal. Drive for 13–16 km (8–10 mi) to the small village of Port Mellon, which the locals call Dogpatch. Take Dunham Road, a right turn immediately after the apartment block on your right, and follow it to the water's edge. Be forewarned that high tide comes well up on the road—you don't want to come back to find your vehicle up to the doors in water.

From this vantage point you are looking across Thornbrough Channel toward Gambier Island, with its smaller neighbour Woolridge Island sitting in front.

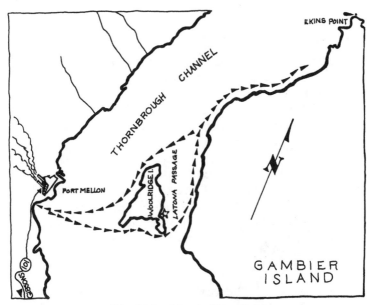

Woolridge Island– Ekins Point

CAUTIONS

Thornbrough Channel is a protected waterway and frequently calm. Nonetheless, winds can whistle up the channel and make for difficult paddling, especially when the tide is against you as well. High seas are rare but winds can produce heavy chop.

Howe Sound is said to have the greatest concentration of log booms anywhere in the world. During working hours, tugs towing huge barges and booms come and go constantly from the busy Port Mellon pulp mill and area booming grounds. You want to treat them with respect. On weekends the commercial traffic subsides, to be replaced with recreational boaters.

Be particularly careful to watch out for "deadheads"—logs that have escaped from booms and taken on water so that they are partly submerged. They are encountered frequently throughout coastal waters, especially in and around booming grounds.

THE TRIP

Woolridge Island is directly across Thornbrough Channel, snuggled up against Gambier Island. Paddle toward the western tip

GREAT BLUE HERON

Franhnk! Franhnk! Franhnk! The morning quiet is broken by the cries of the Great Blue Heron as it glides from its perch above the water, trailing its long legs, neck folded back in a graceful S, to another vantage point farther up the coast. The heron's raucous call contrasts with its calm serenity when it

stands motionless in the shallows, waiting to strike at a variety of fishes and other small aquatic animals.

The Great Blue Heron can grow to 1.2 m (4 feet) tall with an impressive wingspan. These birds are a common sight on trees at the water's edge, in shallows and on log booms.

of Woolridge Island. The coastal mountains are especially splendid from the middle of the channel.

Rocky beaches greet you all along the island shore until you round the point to enter Latona Passage between Woolridge and Gambier islands. Sheer cliffs rise out of the water on either side. Exploring these shorelines at an easy pace, you can enjoy colonies of starfish clustered on the rock face, and soaring cliffs all around, with trees clinging to their craggy surfaces.

The shores of both Gambier and Woolridge islands are booming grounds for the mill, and the shore may be covered with log booms. Herons love these booms. We have seen as many as 10 birds stationed every 60 m (200 feet) on these booms, patiently waiting for lunch to cruise by. Kingfishers swooped between the trees along the shore, and an occasional seal rose out of the water to watch us.

We found it fascinating to watch loggers deftly rounding up logs with a tug. When one of the men left the boat and ran along the logs, we were even more impressed. As we approached for a better look, he suddenly rolled off his log and plunged into the water. Boy, was he furious! The air was blue as we beat a hasty retreat. There is more than one kind of wildlife to see in these waters.

You can relax with a sandwich on a small beach near the southeast tip of Woolridge Island (see asterisk on map). There is a private summer camp on the other side of the sandbar, so stay on the east coast.

Continue the trip by paddling northeast along the eastern arm of Thornbrough Channel toward Ekins Point. How far you go depends on how much time you can spend and how much paddling you want to do.

As you move along the Gambier coast, the cliffs collapse and you can step out on friendlier rocks. Be sure to tether your kayak firmly, then climb to a vantage point to enjoy the view.

On the return trip, paddle straight southwest, leaving Woolridge Island to the left. You will paddle 3.2 km (2 mi) from the northern tip of Woolridge Island back to your launching beach.

TRIP TIME
3 to 6 hours, depending on how much time you take to relax and explore.

GRACE ISLAND AND WEST BAY
GETTING THERE
Start from the launch site in Gibsons Harbour. Stay on the main street of Lower Gibsons as it curves around the waterfront until you reach Headlands Road, then turn left to the water. You will reach a firm sand beach between the marina and the breakwater at the foot of Steep Bluff. Drive onto the beach to unload your gear, then park up on the road. Starting the trip here adds some paddling time.

An alternate launch site is the public pier at Hopkins Landing. Exit the ferry terminal and turn left along Marine Drive toward Gibsons. Just 500 m (.3 mi) from that turn, Hopkins Road branches off on the water side. This road is hard to find, so watch

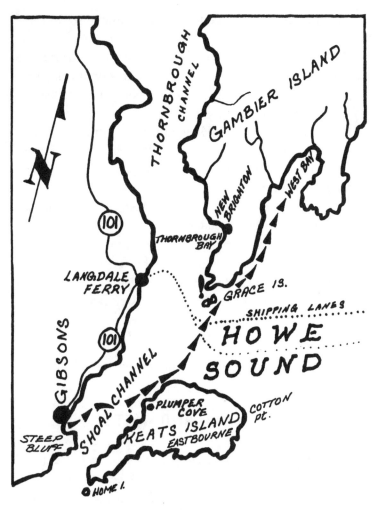

Grace Island–West Bay

carefully. There is a pier and a small beach at the foot of the road.

CAUTIONS

Crossing from the mainland to Gambier Island, you will paddle across the Langdale ferry route and the shipping lane leading to the pulp mill at Port Mellon. It is imperative that you be fully aware of the ferry schedule before setting out. You have an interval of one hour between ferries to make your crossing. Remember that these vessels cannot see you well or take evasive action even if they do know you are there, so proceed with the greatest caution.

As well as the ferry, watch for large tugs and similar commercial vessels coming and going from the mill. The "rules of the road" state that smaller vessels must stay out of the path of these larger boats with their limited manoeuvrability.

Ferry wash is a force to be respected if you are close to shore, where the waves will break or be deflected back and create chop. This wash may be most unexpected and most hazardous to a boat that has been pulled up on shore while you are taking a walk on an otherwise calm day. These large waves can really bounce the boat around, especially the wash from an incoming ferry.

Winds in Thornbrough Channel can also be a hazard, although big seas are not a problem due to the lack of long fetches. In winter, outflow winds can come up rapidly and blow strongly, making paddling difficult.

THE TRIP

Launching from Gibsons Harbour or Hopkins Landing, paddle north along the coast until you are past the ferry terminal. Exercise appropriate caution to avoid the ferries and other commercial traffic. Once clear of this traffic, cross the Channel toward Grace Island, just off the southern tip of Gambier Island. Slip behind the island around the point into West Bay. Paddling down the shoreline of the bay, you will pass towering rock cliffs and occasional beaches. Vistas worthy of picture postcards are a treat for the eye as snow-capped mountains rise out of the water on every side.

If a brisk walk is to your liking, two public wharfs along the shore, Gambier Harbour and West Bay, give you access to the settled areas of the island.

The shores of West Bay carry suggestions of our logging past. Battered concrete posts stand in the shallows, gradually being eroded by the growth invading every crevice. Here you see a rusting cable attached to a tree, there a sagging log ramp sloping into the sea. An ancient barge sits on the beach, slowly wearing down under wind and water.

The very end of the bay finds you at the mouth of a creek, from where you can hear the water tumbling down the mountainside in the winter rainy season. You can stop here and hike a short way up the mountain to see the waterfall coursing through a woods all hung with mosses. This is a possible campsite if you are planning to stay overnight.

Mosses and lichen are a beautiful feature of this shoreline. They grow in great profusion on the rocky cliffs, constantly moistened by the water that seeps down the steep slopes. Along with ferns, the moss and lichen form a study in green textures clinging precariously on narrow ledges of rock.

TRIP TIME
4 to 5 hours. The trip from Gibsons Harbour to Grace Island takes an hour in good conditions. The Hopkins Landing launch site is 30 minutes closer.

THORNBROUGH BAY AND NEW BRIGHTON
GETTING THERE
Launch from Dunham Road, Gibsons Harbour, or Hopkins Landing (see Woolridge Island and Grace Island trips, above).

CAUTIONS
Strong winds can make for difficult paddling, especially when the tide is against you as well. Respect the movement of commercial barge and log boom vessels, and watch out for deadheads (partly submerged logs).

THE TRIP
When you have crossed the channel and reached Gambier

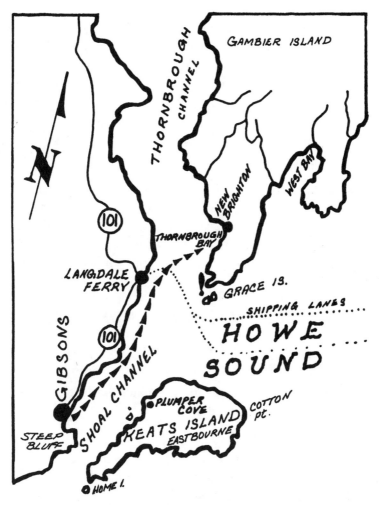

Thornbrough Bay–New Brighton

Island, choose the western shoreline so that you can enjoy a beautiful coast of rocks and trees. You will see summer cottages and permanent dwellings along the whole coast of Gambier, with long stretches of deserted land between.

Thornbrough Bay on the west shore is home to the tiny settlement of New Brighton. Get out of your boat on the public wharf and walk a short way up the hill to a charming general store and restaurant—a stop for lunch here is a must! They feature local arts and crafts, basic supplies and some of the best home baking you have ever tasted.

From New Brighton you can hike to the interior of the island or to Gambier Harbour pier. There is a lovely lake up the mountain which is a favourite hiking destination. Check out the map of the island in front of the store or ask the locals for hiking information.

TRIP TIME
4 to 6 hours, depending on your launch site. The trip from Gibsons Harbour to the island is an hour, with a further 30 minutes to get to New Brighton. Launching from the Hopkins Landing site takes 30 minutes off the time. It takes an hour to get from Dunham Road to New Brighton.

GAMBIER ISLAND EXTENDED TRIPS

HALKETT BAY PROVINCIAL PARK
GETTING THERE
Launch from Gibsons Harbour or Hopkins Landing (see Grace Island and West Bay trip, above).

CAUTIONS
To reach Halkett Bay you will be crossing commercial lanes in both Thornbrough and Collingwood channels. Check the map to familiarize yourself with the shipping lanes before you start out. Know the ferry schedule, stay out of the way of larger vessels, and obey all the rules of the road.

Outflow winds from the coastal mountains are a force to be reckoned with in Howe Sound. The Squamish winds originate at the head of the Sound, come up quickly and reach high  velocities. They normally blow down Montagu Channel, then fan out between Queen Charlotte Channel,

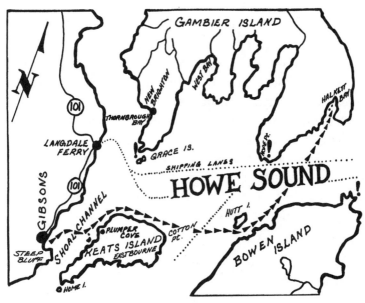

Halkett Bay Provincial Park

Collingwood Channel and Barfleur Passage (see overview map, page 40). These winds are strongest in the winter months when cold air pours out of the high mountains like water from a pitcher.

In summer, the winds are gentler. The good-weather westerlies blow up Barfleur Passage, reaching the end of that fetch at the southeast point of Gambier Island, so look for the heaviest seas of the trip as you cross Collingwood Channel. The wise paddler will stop off Cotton Point on Keats Island to assess the situation before making the crossing. These daily winds tend to subside in late afternoon, so plan accordingly.

THE TRIP

Beginning in Gibsons Harbour, paddle across Shoal Channel and around the north side of Keats Island. The towering peaks of the coastal mountains open out before you in a magnificent vista. Hugging the coast of Keats allows you to enjoy the various kinds of starfish that cling to the rocky shores.

Collingwood Channel is a favourite spot for viewing wildlife of all kinds due to its brisk tidal flows. Watch for birds, seals and the occasional whale.

From Cotton Point, head across to Hutt Island where you can slip into the lee of the island for a rest before venturing across to Gambier. The shortest crossing to the island starts here, but head for a point east of Hope Point, on the southeast end of Gambier, to stay in the lee of Bowen.

Halkett Bay is then a short paddle down the coast. This Provincial Marine Park has wonderful campsites. From here you can explore the eastern face of Gambier Island and enjoy its wonderful variety of seascapes.

TRIP TIME
At least 2 days to complete the trip. It is a good 4-hour paddle to Halkett Bay.

DOUGLAS BAY AND BRIGADE BAY
GETTING THERE
You can reach Douglas and Brigade bays from Port Mellon. Turn right on Dunham Road just past the apartment block on your right, and follow it to the water's edge. From there you will paddle through protected waters to the bays on the east face of Gambier Island.

Should you have time to circumnavigate Gambier, you can paddle in either direction depending on conditions at the start of the trip. There are four campsites on the perimeter of Gambier: Douglas Bay, Brigade Bay, Halkett Bay and West Bay.

Of these, only Halkett Bay is a government park. The others are part of logging areas of the island, commonly used but not public lands.

CAUTIONS
The back side of Gambier is thoroughly protected but subject to local winds. Ramillies Channel lies in the lee of Anvil

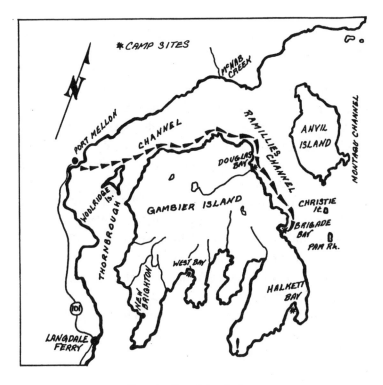

Douglas Bay–Brigade Bay

Island, shielding it from the worst of the outflow winds. Occasional outflows originate in the McNab and Potlatch creeks, primarily in the fall and winter. Obey the rules of the road.

Winds can be hazardous on the crossing to Anvil Island, especially the area around Christie Islet and Pam Rock, so pick the time and day carefully.

After the crossing to Gambier Island, this trip is mainly shoreline paddling in protected waters.

THE TRIP

Paddle toward Woolridge Island, and continue to the east side of Gambier Island, opposite Anvil Island. This side of Gambier is spectacular, with rock cliffs soaring out of the sea against a backdrop of towering coastal mountains. This area is devoted

55

to logging leases and so is mostly uninhabited. Seabirds abound in these quiet waters and seals fish the channels in large numbers.

Camp on the shoreline in either Douglas Bay or Brigade Bay under a canopy of gigantic broadleaf maples, and enjoy the peace and tranquility of the outdoors on the doorstep of Vancouver. There is a particularly attractive waterfall beside the Douglas Bay site, and from Brigade Bay you can enjoy a splendid hike up the hill behind the site.

If weather permits, a trip to Christie Islet and Pam Rock is a delight. This tiny islet and sprinkling of bare rocks, poking out of the water just south of Anvil Island, are home to one of our largest seal colonies. They are also breeding grounds for Glaucous-winged Gulls and cormorants. Harlequin Ducks, Hooded Mergansers, Bonaparte's Gulls and many others can be seen in their seasons. Double-crested Cormorants have been building their nests of twigs on these rocks for many years and now they are 2- or 3-foot-high structures perched on the rocky ledges. A most unusual sight!

TRIP TIME

So many variations are possible on this trip that they cannot be counted. Gibsons Harbour to Halkett Bay is 4 good hours of paddling, and Dunham Road to Douglas Bay is about 3 hours. Using these times as a guideline, plan each leg of your trip to the time you have available.

From Gibsons Harbour around Gambier and back again is approximately 41.5 km (26 mi). Expect to paddle about 5 km/h (3 mph) if you are moving at a relaxed pace and stopping to enjoy the sights. Paddling time will also depend on the direction of the tide and wind.

South Howe Sound

PLUMPER COVE, KEATS ISLAND

GETTING THERE

Start from the launch site at Gibsons Harbour. Follow the main street of Lower Gibsons around the waterfront, turn left at Headlands Road and follow it to a firm sand beach just beyond the marina and inside the breakwater, at the foot of Steep Bluff. Drive your vehicle on the beach to unload your gear, but remember to park up on the road.

This is one of the easiest launching sites on the whole coast, as it places you at water's edge in all conditions. It is also handy to hot coffee and food upon your return.

CAUTIONS

Shoal Channel and the harbour at Gibsons are in such a well-protected area that you may be completely oblivious to hazardous conditions in the Strait of Georgia. The gap leading to the strait is a shallow spot, and any waves will pick up dramatically here. We have paddled through some pretty heavy seas on leaving the harbour that were not evident at all when we entered the water.

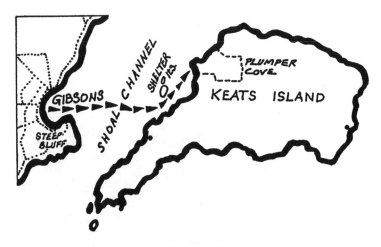

Plumper Cove

In summer, the westerly sea breezes of the afternoon may affect you as you cross from Steep Bluff to Keats Island. In winter, the Squamish winds are of concern here.

Be careful to watch for heavy commercial and recreational boat traffic when paddling in the channels. Ferry wash is another factor to consider.

THE TRIP

Once you have launched from Gibsons Harbour, a number of alternative routes to Plumper Cove Provincial Park are available. You may want to paddle north along the coast to see Gibsons and its environs before crossing the channel.

Or you can head directly to Plumper Cove from the launch site. This is a crossing of about 1.6 km (1 mi) over open water, another chance to savour the splendour of the coastal mountains as you bob along like so much flotsam.

If the channel is windy, you may prefer to go south around Steep Bluff, cross the narrow channel to Keats and follow the shore to the park.

When you slip into the cove behind the Shelter Islets, the

public wharf and the park are before you. Hiking trails follow the coast and wind through the forest—a birdwatcher's delight.

The park is a popular visiting spot for boaters of all kinds, so don't expect solitude in the summer months. On the other hand, you will meet plenty of nice folks who love to share stories of their seafaring adventures.

TRIP TIME
3 hours is ample time for this trip.

KEATS ISLAND CIRCUMNAVIGATION
GETTING THERE
Launch from Gibsons Harbour (see Plumper Cove trip, above).

CAUTIONS
Weather conditions on the open strait may not be obvious from the protection of the harbour, so look to the forecast before setting out.

West winds will be augmented by the funnelling and channelling effect through the gap between the mainland and Keats Island.

Gibsons Harbour at sunset   Keith Thirkell photo

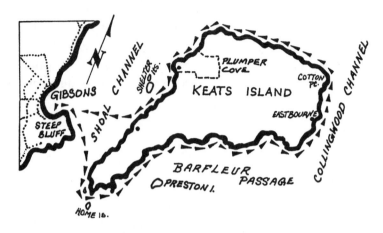

Keats Island Circumnavigation

Collingwood Channel at the east end of Keats will be affected by the southeast winds and the westerlies.

THE TRIP

Proceed south around Steep Bluff, and head out of the harbour and toward Home Island at the south tip of Keats.

Shoal Channel is an area of increased wave action due to the funnelling effect and the shallow water. When you reach a tiny cove behind the rocks off the southern tip of Keats, the tumult suddenly subsides. A pocket beach gives you an opportunity to rest or hike a bit—a particularly nice place to watch the sunset. This little cove is dry at lowest tides but offers a safe harbour when the water depth permits.

Once you turn northeast along the southern face of the island, you are protected from the winds and the paddling is easy and pleasant.

This is an excellent area for off-season paddling, thanks to its proximity to the comforts of home. Great flocks of seabirds winter off this coast. Scoters start away with whistling wings when you get too close, their fat, black rumps just barely clearing the surface of the water.

For the next mile or so, the shoreline is sparsely settled and you can enjoy a taste of wilderness solitude. There are a couple of rocky beaches in small bays along the coast where you can get out of your boat. The swimming is great in the summer.

This is a nice stretch of coast to drift along quietly, observing the life of the water, woods and shore. You will see loons aplenty, kingfishers swooping from tree to tree, eagles watching from their favourite snags and, of course, the ever-present gulls. On one trip we surprised a raccoon in the act of washing his food at the edge of the water. His curiosity kept him there as we drifted quietly past.

Keats Island

Toward the east end of the island, the settlement of East-bourne appears. You can park your boat at the small beach beside the public wharf, while you take a walk along the roads that meander through the community.

Continuing to paddle around the island, you will round Cotton Point and move along the northern shore, facing Thorn-brough Channel. From your tiny craft tucked up against the shoreline, the ferry is massive and majestic as it passes.

There are no beaches for the next mile or so. Rocky shores drop straight into deep water and the trees hang right over your head from time to time.

Just before turning south into Shoal Channel, you will see a farm on the shore, where cows graze placidly in quiet pastures. The pier is often alive with children in the summer.

Plumper Cove Provincial Park (see above), another good place to stretch your legs, comes next.

On calm days paddle directly across the channel to enjoy

The Aqua Nauts

*Their destination the Pasleys, placed a mile open water
crossing before them.
A low pressure front hung as leaden liquid veils.
Westerlies increasing in power began sweeping the sea surface
churning swells to dumping white caps.
On the dark horizon a patch is torn open exposing blue sky
The high front was advancing with accelerated aggression.
On reaching the islands a hasty return was agreed upon.
Billowing clouds reaching monolithic proportions
dwarf their world below.
Ever increasing winds cause waves to explode.
Chilling waters wash over their tiny craft spraying exposed flesh.
Wet, tired and triumphant they paddle into
the quiet waters of Gibsons harbour
completing a journey through the war zone
of opposing weather fronts.*

fabulous views of mountains, town and water. This crossing is a good 1.5 km (1 mi) and will take you about 20 or 30 minutes.

As an alternative, you may wish to continue along the coast of Keats until you reach the narrower crossing. Winds and tides will dictate your decision.

TRIP TIME

About 4 hours including a couple of leisurely stops. To circle the island you will paddle about 13 km (8 mi) in safe, well-protected waters for the most part.

THE PASLEY ISLANDS

GETTING THERE

Launch from Gibsons Harbour (see Plumper Cove, above).

CAUTIONS

Be aware that seas will pick up in Shoal Channel due to the shallow water there.

Barfleur Passage between Keats Island and the Pasleys funnels westerlies into Howe Sound and outflow winds blow from the mountains, so this crossing can be pretty windy. Check conditions before starting out and before the return trip. The islands look so close but they are really a good mile offshore.

THE TRIP

Head around Steep Bluff and make the crossing to Home Island off the tip of Keats.

Now set out across Barfleur Passage toward the Pasley Islands just south of you. The long fetch to the west can produce some good seas here. We have had some exhilarating paddles crossing to these islands.

Head for Popham Island, the most westerly of the group. Seals are frequently seen fishing the passage between Popham and Little Popham or lounging on the rocky shoals at the western extremity of the island. Remember to stay at least

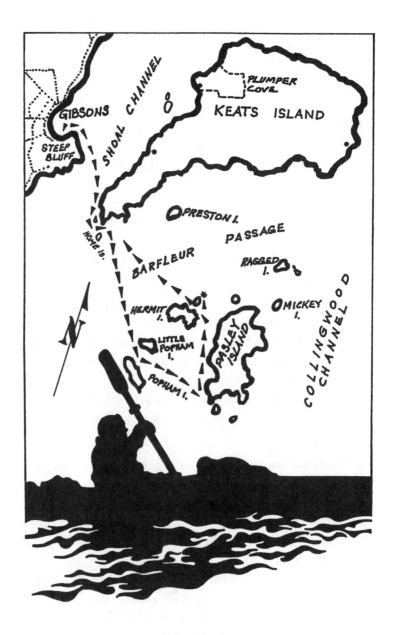

Pasley Islands

MARBLED MURRELET

This unpretentious little bird has become the focus of the fight to save old-growth forests, as it nests exclusively in this habitat. A chubby little bird with a very short neck, it is seen in summer, usually alone or in a pair, diving for prey in bays and inlets all up and down the Sunshine Coast. Summer plumage is soft marbled brown and white below with dark brown above, while in winter the bird is white below and black above with a white stripe where the wings meet the back.

100 m (110 yds) off the shore to protect the well-being of the colony, especially the pups in spring.

Once in the environs of the islands, you are protected from the full force of the winds and are free to explore the varied shorelines at your leisure.

The Pasley Islands are all privately owned, so please show respect for the residents. They have designated the small islet just north of Hermit Island, the northernmost island, as a picnic area and resting spot for visitors. It is a pleasant little area with nice beaches, rocks on the shore and a tiny forest of arbutus covering its centre.

In spite of the human population, there is a wealth of bird life in the waters around the islands—mergansers, Harlequin Ducks, cormorants, kingfishers and the flocks of tiny birds that frequent the brush on many shorelines.

Pasley Island lies in the centre with a necklace of smaller islands surrounding it. The shores are all rocky, most falling into deep water right at the edge. There are few beaches but many landing opportunities on the low rocks.

Spend as much time as you wish exploring these islands.

But keep an eye on the weather, as Barfleur Passage is quite exposed and the return trip can be challenging.

TRIP TIME

4 hours minimum. Leave at least 2 hours for crossing to the islands and back, and at least 2 more hours to explore the area.

BOWEN ISLAND EXTENDED TRIP

GETTING THERE

Launch from Gibsons Harbour (see Plumper Cove, page 57).

CAUTIONS

Wind is the worst hazard you will face on this trip. The good-weather westerlies and outflow winds from the interior will affect you when crossing both Barfleur Passage and Collingwood Channel. The campsite and launch site on Bowen face west, so are exposed to the west wind.

These waterways are not travelled as heavily as the ferry route, but they are shipping lanes. Exercise caution.

The south coast of Bowen is characterized by high cliffs with few landing spots. It is fully exposed to the southeasterly winds that usher in a change in the weather and the good-weather westerlies. Expect lots of confused seas as the waves are deflected off the cliffs.

THE TRIP

Head around Steep Bluff and make the crossing to Home Island off the tip of Keats.

Now set out across Barfleur Passage, to the eastern end of Worlcombe Island, then paddle toward Bowen Island, heading for the light on Cape Roger Curtis.

As you draw near you will see a small beach almost hidden by large rocks, with a steep wooded cliff behind. To the right is a lovely, flat, grassy area ideal for camping. The rocks in front shield the small landing area even on windy days.

This little beach is great for swimming and launching but

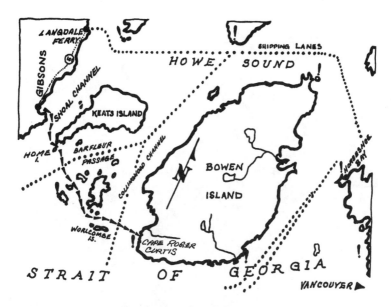

Bowen Island Extended Trip

is almost completely covered at high tide, so don't leave your gear here—you will never see it again. The hills behind are crisscrossed with old logging trails, used by many hikers and bikers.

You now have a base to explore the outer coast of Bowen before returning to Gibsons.

TRIP TIME

3 hours of paddling will easily get you to Cape Roger Curtis. For strong paddlers this trip is a day trip, but if you'd rather not paddle that far in a day, this is an ideal trip for a weekend.

Canada Geese, Trail Island in background   Keith Thirkell photo

Sechelt

Northwest toward Sechelt, Highway 101 winds gently through the semi-rural settlement that blankets the coast. Homes and businesses give way to forests. Plazas and auto dealers appear in their turn. Just after you cross the Chapman Creek bridge, the road breaks out onto the seashore at Mission Point. This gentle arc of beach on the east side of Trail Bay is called Davis Bay.

Take a look around from this vantage point. A wide sandy beach stretches before you at low tide, and to the south, bare rocks rise from the sea offshore. These are the White Islets.

Around the corner to the left, Chapman Creek spills into the sea, giving the water that oily look that occurs when salt water and fresh water mix. Great flocks of gulls, sea ducks and shorebirds congregate on the spit at the creek mouth.

This beach is perhaps the most widely used on the coast, with the sharp smell of suntan lotion filling the air on hot summer days. Children dart across the road to get goodies from the shops, so drive carefully here.

The triangle of sea that is Trail Bay unfolds to the right. At its tip is Sechelt, with the Trail Islands scattered over the sea to the west—four peaks poking through the surface surrounded by their shoals, each wearing a brush cut of forest on its brow.

THE WHITE ISLETS

GETTING THERE

From the Langdale ferry terminal, follow Highway 101 through Gibsons northwest toward Sechelt. Finding your launch site is no problem here. Just park in the small lot off the highway at Mission Point, at the south end of Davis Bay, and launch from the beach. What could be easier?

CAUTIONS

Wind is the big problem in this area. No islands intercede between you and the long fetches of the Strait of Georgia. All the prevailing winds blow onto these shores unobstructed. Be sure of your weather before setting out, and keep a sharp eye out for changes.

The islets are almost 3 km (2 mi) offshore but often look much closer. This is a good example of the difficulty of judging distance over water. Don't be fooled by appearances.

This islet is a bird sanctuary so you *must* not land on its shores during the breeding season, which runs from spring through early summer.

GLAUCOUS-WINGED GULL

These are large white gulls with soft grey over wings and back, a strong yellow beak with a red spot on the underside, pink feet and a voracious appetite for almost anything edible. Their familiar call is everywhere evocative of the sea.

There are breeding colonies of these gulls on rocky islets along the coast. In early summer you will see little brown balls squatting patiently in a rock crevice waiting for their parents to return with the next meal. Remember that panic behaviour among the adult birds can destroy eggs and chicks, so keep your distance.

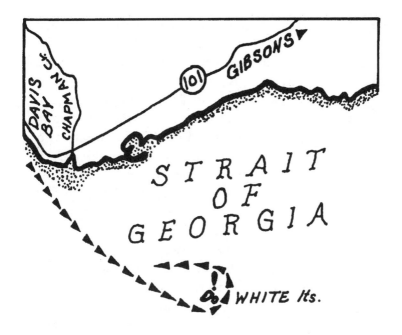

White Islets

Some of the most interesting sights can be seen in winter, but weather conditions are extremely variable at this time. Exercise extra caution.

At high tide the sand is covered, and you will launch on a cobble beach. In windy conditions, you may want to paddle up Chapman Creek a bit to save the bottom of your boat.

THE TRIP

No complicated directions here, just launch from the beach at the south end of Davis Bay. At the mouth of Chapman Creek you will see lots of bird life. All the local varieties of gulls hang out here in large numbers so expect to see large Glaucous-winged Gulls, the smaller Herring Gulls and the delicate little Bonaparte's Gulls all mixed together.

When you have had your fill of this area, head out for the islets south of Mission Point. During the crossing you will be treated to a panoramic view of the coast: mountains rising on the near side and Vancouver Island far across the strait. Watch for eagles; one day we counted some fifty eagles perched on the rocks or flying above us. Summer finds family groups only, but large numbers of these birds congregate here in winter.

One April day we paddled out. The sun was hot in spite of the season, and a stiff breeze from the southeast made for a brisk workout. As we approached the islet, a cacophony of bird sounds greeted us from gulls, Sanderlings, Black Turnstones and Canada Geese. As we approached, the shorebirds swooped away as one body, tails and wings flashing white, then dark. We could hear and feel the whir of their collective wings as they passed.

Approaching from the beach, you see only a large rock outcrop with no trees and bits of vegetation struggling out of crevices. A marine light perches on the crest of the rock. Seaward from this largest islet is a smaller bit of rock. In early spring each year, migrating Steller's and California Sea Lions stop on these rocks. Their quarrelsome bellowing, announcing their presence to all, can be heard from land. When threatened, these animals can get cranky, as we learned on our first trip out to see them. In our ignorance we pulled around the seaward corner to find ourselves right beside the haulout. Startled, the whole herd hit the water while the bulls lined up in front of us, posturing aggressively and barking. It gives you pause to have an enormous critter snarling at you from close range. We backed off quickly and on subsequent trips stayed that 100 m (330 feet) out. The seals that inhabit these shores the rest of the year find alternative lodgings during the visit of the sea lions.

One nice December morning, we tried to sneak up on the islands to catch the seals unawares. To no avail—they hit the water long before we got near. It is frustrating to watch them ignore a sailboat passing close by, while we generate such suspicion. Someone suggested that in our boats we may look like the long, thin dorsal fins of a killer whale rising out of the water. Or maybe the seals are just more accustomed to the passing of larger boats.

We saw lots of seals that day but only a few sea lions. A huge bull with a coat of deep red-brown hair lumbered awkwardly into the water at our approach. He cruised languidly off shore, one flipper sticking straight out of the water, then rolled over and up came the other flipper. He was a most impressive size but pretty mild mannered at that time of year. Another sea lion flipped a large salmon into the air just in front of our boats while farther out a pair rolled about in the water, then reared up to look at us as we passed. These creatures seem to like to entertain visitors in their range.

It is pretty easy to distinguish the male from the female of this species—the males are much bigger with large, bulbous snouts. As the season approaches, you see one or two, then small groups at various sites along the coast. Eventually there will be up to fifty animals crowded on the islet for a time.

Both seals and sea lions hang out on the smaller rocks behind the largest islet, unseen as you paddle toward them. Approach from either the seaward or the landward side, keeping

Sea lions, White Islets

a good distance from the islet to get the best view of these fascinating animals.

There are also flocks of Surfbirds and Black Turnstones here, foraging along the shore. They are friendly little creatures that will go about their business as if oblivious to your presence if you approach them delicately. A flock in flight behaves as one organism, weaving and darting in perfect tandem.

One day we noted a ducklike bird hunkered down on the rocks. He was coal black with a white flash on his wing, and we had never seen his like before. Rising to his feet, he squawked, startling us with the bright red on his feet and the lining of his beak. He was a Pigeon Guillemot, one of the less common seabirds found along the coast.

TRIP TIME

About 2 ½ hours total. It takes 20 to 30 minutes to make the crossing to the islets.

THE TRAIL ISLANDS

GETTING THERE

Two launch sites in Sechelt both offer access to the waters of Trail Bay.

The first is the boat ramp in Selma Park, the neighbourhood on the south side of Sechelt. Watch for the Boat Ramp sign between Davis Bay and Sechelt and turn off the highway there. A concrete ramp and a small beach behind a breakwater offer good parking and protected access to the water. The islands lie almost 3 km (2 mi) away across Trail Bay.

To reach the second site, Wakefield Creek, drive past

Pigeon Guillemots

Sechelt along Highway 101 for approximately 3 km (2 mi). Watch for glimpses of the Trails through the trees as you drive. Mason Road and West Sechelt climb the hill beside you on the right, and about 15 m

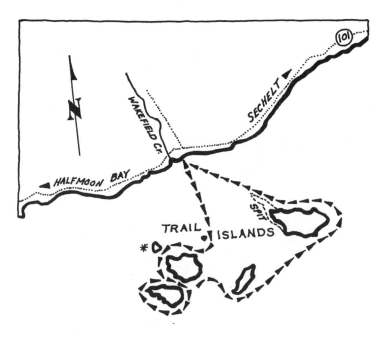

Trail Islands

(50 feet) farther is a short, unmarked road down to the water. Take this road and follow it to a small parking area at the end. Immediately west is a large white bubble structure (an indoor tennis court) and then the Wakefield Inn. If you pass this local watering hole you've gone too far. This launch site is a good choice in nice weather or when you don't want to traverse the bay. The islands are .8 km (.5 mi) away, an easy paddle.

CAUTIONS

The hazard here is wind. The prevailing winds of the Strait of Georgia—westerlies in summer and southeasterlies in winter—are often at their strongest along the Sunshine Coast, especially in areas like this, where the coast is exposed to long fetches to the north and south.

The daily sea breezes that occur on sunny, warm days will augment the good weather westerlies. They come up by 10:00 in the morning and can reach 20 knots or more by early afternoon. As the winds tend to abate by 4:00 p.m., wait it out if necessary.

The islands will shelter the Wakefield Creek launch site from the southeasterlies to some extent, but westerlies cause heavy chop in this area. The channel between the islands and the mainland is shallow so waves will become steeper here. Similarly, the paddle across Trail Bay from Selma Park will keep you in the lee of the islands during west winds but expose you to the full force of southeast winds.

THE TRIP

The Trail Islands have provided us with many delightful days on the water. These islands are home to an astonishing array of wildlife. Two seal colonies lounge on their haulouts at low tide. Most will take to the water at your approach, then follow you with every indication of great curiosity. If you don't push too hard, the patriarchs stick to their posts, watching disdainfully as you glide past.

Paddle directly across to the rocks just east of the two most westerly islands. Low tide will find the seals resting on the rocks, while high tides send them to their favourite feeding spots around the islands. Cormorants often gather here as well, perched at the water's edge with their wings hanging out to dry.

We usually check out these two westernmost islands first as they offer the greatest variety in wildlife. A second seal colony lives on the rocks off their western tip, and eagles like this spot as well. Drifting along the shore you will enjoy observing a variety of land and marine life.

The small bare islet (marked with an asterisk on the map) makes a good rest stop during most of the year. As it sits in the lee of two larger islands, you will find the calm waters necessary for you to clamber out on the rocks and sit quietly watching the activity in the area. Canada Geese like to raise families in this spot, so stay off in the spring.

We never fail to explore the narrow channel separating the

two westerly islands. The faster-flowing water enhances the growth of sea life and draws all the local denizens to this spot. One early spring day we counted six eagles sitting in the snags on either side. Most were juveniles but a couple had the white heads of adult eagles. Harlequin Ducks regularly cruise this passage, diving for food at the margins.

On a cliff at the seaward end of this narrow channel, a nesting colony of Pelagic Cormorants perches precariously on narrow ledges, bits of seaweed tumbled in willy nilly, with flags of white droppings marking their spot. They nest on such tight spots that they must take off and land facing the cliff. These birds make the most unusual sounds around breeding colonies. As you draw near, eerie groaning and sighing noises fill the air. The usual admonitions to give space to families are in order here.

Glaucous-winged Gulls raise families on the seaward cliffs of the Trails. These birds can travel long distances to find food for their nestlings. Both parents defend the nest vigorously. You may see the little round balls of light brown fluff sitting in the nesting area, patiently waiting for food.

Heading out to the Trail Islands.

Paddling amongst the Trails, you can cruise along in the lee of the islands fully protected from the winds, or test your skills in more challenging waters by sprinting around the seaward side to play in the waves. Be aware that the waves here are confused and turbulent as they are repelled from steep cliffs, and there are no landing spots on the outer shores. Not a good time to find that your reach has exceeded your grasp.

The smallest island of this group, rising almost equidistant between its larger neighbours, has steep cliffs on all sides. Look for starfish colonies and other underwater creatures at low tide.

A short paddle to the east brings you to the largest of the islands. The southeast tip of the island is uninhabited at this time so we landed there and took a short walk along the shoreline. The cliffs are quite precipitous, limiting the distance we could walk, but they provide a nice lookout over the Strait of Georgia. It's a great spot for lunch.

Along the seaward side, massive blocks of rock are stacked in piles, rising out of deep water like a giant stairway. The delicate pinks, blues and greys of the rocks are reflected in the ever-moving sea, all worn smooth by the water's unceasing rhythm.

There is a long spit of rock and gravel reaching shoreward from its northwest point. We watched the tide running across the spit one day and wondered at the power and beauty of the patterns these forces created on the water's surface. A flock of oystercatchers stabbed the rocks with their strong red beaks, darting here and there in the relentless search for food. We once saw almost fifty of these birds on this spit. Seals often hang out here too.

TRIP TIME

35 to 40 minutes to cross from Selma Park to the islands, and less than 20 minutes to paddle from Wakefield Creek to the islands. Then spend as much time as you like exploring this fascinating area.

Sechelt Inlet

The word Sechelt is derived from the name of a local First Nations village, *Se-shalt*, meaning "a place of shelter from the sea." As you approach Sechelt, you pass through the lands of the Sechelt, a Coast Salish group who were the first Native band in Canada to achieve self-government. Their pride in their accomplishments is reflected in the Band Administration Building, prominent on your left as you drive into town from the south. Take this opportunity to explore the museum, which displays many interesting artifacts from the region.

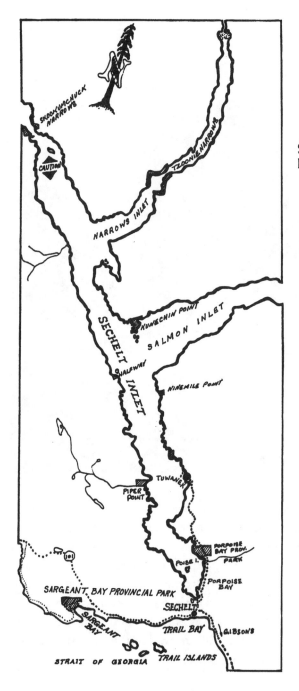

Sechelt
Inlet

A perfect day on Sechelt Inlet

At the first traffic lights, a left turn on Wharf Street takes you to the main street of town and on up the coast. To the right is Porpoise Bay Road and the Sechelt Inlet.

Downtown Sechelt sits on a narrow peninsula—less than a mile wide—that separates the Sechelt Inlet from the Strait of Georgia. Schemes to join these two bodies of water by building a mini-Panama Canal surface in the local body politic from time to time. Fortunately they sink without a trace when the enormity of the undertaking hits.

Sechelt is a hub of economic activity on the lower coast, a centre for logging, fishing and an active tourist industry. Visitors are invited to browse through displays of local arts and crafts, drink cappuccino on an outdoor terrace, enjoy a wide variety of restaurants and stock up at the many shops in town.

The map of the area looks like some ancient hieroglyph, with the long finger of the Sechelt Inlet running northwest from Sechelt, through the Sechelt Rapids in the Skookumchuck Narrows to Jervis Inlet, and two narrow bodies of water reaching out of the inlet to the east. Salmon Inlet is the southerly and the larger of these, and Narrows Inlet lies to the north.

The south end of the Sechelt Inlet, Porpoise Bay, is characterized by long tidal flats that dry at low tide. Homes, marinas and businesses border the shore, sharing the space with a wealth of bird and marine life. As you look out from the government wharf, Poise Island rises to the left. On the east side of the inlet the road ends at Tuwanek and the concentration of human activities ends with it. Here you will see an occasional summer home, some logging on the hillsides and a couple of oyster farms.

The Sechelt Inlet and its associated inlets provide some delightful paddling experiences. Sheltered from the winds of the Strait by the surrounding hills and free from any severe tidal currents, this inland sea offers a wide variety of options for paddlers of all skill levels.

Boaters can enjoy eight marine park sites situated on these shores. Development is limited to signs, sanitary facilities and rustic campsites. Some sites are still completely undeveloped.

Steep cliffs falling straight to the sea, interspersed with a few small bays, characterize the shores of Salmon Inlet. Because of the inhospitable shoreline and tendency to wind, it is not as favoured by the paddling community as Narrows Inlet to the northwest. Those with good paddling skills and the yen for a challenge will find some spectacular trips on Salmon Inlet. Expect to paddle fairly long distances between landing spots. The park at Thornhill Creek is suitable for camping.

Narrows Inlet is a lovely, gentle place, so narrow that it feels like a broad river. Mountains rise on both sides, capped with snow in the cooler seasons. Streams rush down the steep slopes, creating spectacular waterfalls over the lower cliffs, especially in the rainy seasons.

At Tzoonie Narrows the inlet narrows drastically, creating a tidal rapid of 4 knots at its height. Such spots with increased water flow favour the growth of marine creatures, so look for life

Narrows Inlet

in the water here. Many varieties of wildlife inhabit the area. From mountain goats to bears to seals, sky, land and water are alive with interesting creatures to see and enjoy.

Besides the provincial campground, Narrows Inlet offers a couple of well-appointed, private accommodations.

PORPOISE BAY AND POISE ISLAND

GETTING THERE

Turn right at the traffic lights in Sechelt and drive a few short blocks down Wharf Road to the water. A public wharf, a pub and airline terminal line up along the waterfront, backed by a large parking lot. Use the boat launch ramp to enter the water. Be gentle with the kayak on concrete.

CAUTIONS

The few hazards in this area come mainly from human activity and, of course, wind. Seaplanes take off from the government wharf across the stretch of water to Poise Island. Fishing boats and a wide variety of private craft are constantly coming and going here.

Winds in the mid-afternoon can be strong, especially in the summer, but high seas rarely result due to the protected nature of these waters. When paddling here you will notice that the wind direction is extremely variable over very short stretches due to the configuration of the inlet. In windy weather, the western shore offers the most protection.

THE TRIP

Paddle up the western side of the bay, keeping well out of the path of planes and large vessels. The rocks and mud flats of this shoreline are home to a wide variety of marine life. Watch for

rock crabs, several types of starfish, and many schools of small fish. Small bottom fish dart away in puffs of silt, defying the eye to register the details of their appearance. The behaviour suggests flounder, sole or even halibut. The waving fields of eelgrass are favoured hangouts for crabs, especially in the spring breeding season.

One fall day as we crossed from Poise Island, we paddled over acres of jellyfish undulating gently in the clear waters. They filled the water from top to bottom like stars hanging in the firmament. These transparent bells with their trailing filaments invite the hand to touch them, but don't yield to the temptation—they sting.

Take some time to drift around Poise Island observing the marine life off its shores. As the island is privately owned you are not invited to land and explore, but the shoreline offers much of interest for the student of nature. Starfish love these rocky shores, and some of them reach awesome proportions. The sunflower star is the largest intertidal starfish on this coast. The textured, almost furry, blue-grey surface nearly hides the glow of orange emanating from its centre.

Continuing north on the western shore, you'll find the town ends at Snake Bay, but this is changing fast as Sechelt grows. There are a couple of nice beaches on the far side of the bay, a great spot for swimming. Canada Geese also enjoy these beaches and congregate in large numbers here.

In the spring of 1991, half of J Pod—a resident pod of orca whales from the Strait of Georgia—entered the Inlet through the Skookumchuck and spent 12 days cruising Porpoise Bay. Their favourite run was from Snake Bay to Poise Island and back. Each evening local residents lined the bay, on both land and water, to watch these whales feeding and cavorting. Egmont residents report that whales enter the inlet every year in small numbers, but it was most unusual to see a large group stay so far down for such a long time. We paddled to the area on a couple of evenings to enjoy this rare treat. Being so close to these

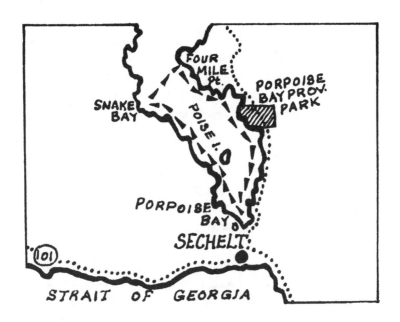

Porpoise Bay–Poise Island

splendid creatures engenders feelings of awe and respect for their power and grace.

Across the Inlet from Snake Bay you see Four Mile Point, its shores covered by the homes of the community of Sandy Hook. Paddle across and return to the launch site via the eastern shore of Porpoise Bay. That shore supports a variety of commercial activity, lots of log sort sites, marinas and the like.

Porpoise Bay Provincial Park, covering 61 ha (150 acres) of the east side of the Sechelt Inlet, stands out as a snippet of forest relieving a well-populated shoreline. The broad sand beach invites you to get out and stretch your legs, and the beach gives way to open, grassy areas backed up by a second-growth forest of Douglas fir, western red cedar, western hemlock, maple and alder. Angus Creek is a spawning stream for Chum and Coho salmon. In the fall of each year, hiking trails along its banks allow an opportunity to view returning fish. This is a nice place to stay, as it is a full-service camp with flush toilets and hot showers.

A leisurely paddle puts you back where you started with ample time to enjoy the pub if you wish.

TRIP TIME
4 to 5 hours.

Alternate trip: PIPER POINT

If you continue up the western side of the inlet from Snake Bay, there is even more to enjoy. At Carleson Creek you will see a homestead established by two women, authentic pioneers who fished, logged and hunted in the area for years. Just beyond that at Piper Point, a small, undeveloped provincial park with a nice little beach provides another good opportunity to land for rest and relaxation.

Retrace your route or cross to the eastern shore and follow it back to the launch site.

TRIP TIME
6 hours, with some periods of steady paddling.

BLACK OYSTERCATCHER

This exotic species has a long, heavy, bright red beak, a chunky black body and red legs and feet. A close encounter reveals bright yellow eyes encircled with red. It forages for small mussels, crustaceans, worms and other organisms along the shore. In summer, Black Oystercatchers nest on the high gravel beaches or rocky promontories of islets where their eggs, gray with dull black spots, are difficult to see even though the

nests are exposed. We once watched a mother sitting on her eggs on an exposed rock in a channel. She blended in to her surroundings so well that only the noisy comings and goings of her mate revealed her to us.

NINE MILE POINT

GETTING THERE

Turn right at the first set of traffic lights in Sechelt and drive 3 blocks to Porpoise Bay Road on your right. This road winds along the eastern side of the inlet, ending at Tuwanek. A small spit reaches out into the bay toward the Lamb Islets, a popular scuba diving spot that is easy to get to and offers an interesting diving experience. An old wolf eel that lives down there entertains those who invade his territory.

Parking space is limited here, so be aware that local residents will object if too many vehicles congest their summer hideaway. Moderation in all things is the order of the day to maintain good relations.

An alternate place to park and launch is Lamb Bay. The turnoff for the bay is at the top of the hill before the main road drops down to the water. Look for a gravel road to the left.

A third option is to launch from Sandy Hook. Turn off Porpoise Bay Road on Sandy Hook Road and wind your way to its end. There you will find a small park with parking lot, sanitary facilities and a nice beach from which to launch. If you launch from here, add another half hour of paddling to reach Salmon Inlet.

CAUTIONS

Wind is a force to be reckoned with in this area. The daily thermal winds begin by mid-morning and generally blow up the inlet until late afternoon. To avoid this hassle, paddle before they start in the morning and return after they moderate in the afternoon.

The mouth of Salmon Inlet is the most hazardous spot on the inlet besides the rapids at Skookumchuck Narrows. The winds of the two inlets meet here, generating confused waters. The length of the fetch can produce 1- to 1.2-m (3- to 4-foot) chop.

Salmon Inlet is bounded by steep cliffs on both sides for most of its length, creating a funnel effect that intensifies the winds. Should you decide to paddle up Salmon Inlet past Nine Mile Point, be aware that landing beaches are few and far between and winds can be very strong.

THE TRIP

Paddling from Tuwanek along the eastern shore of Sechelt Inlet, you leave human habitation behind at once. The Lamb Islets just off Tuwanek are private property, but it is interesting to poke around the edges in your boat.

Tuwanek Point is a short 20-minute paddle from the end of the road. This provincial marine park has a great beach, making it a lovely place to swim and walk. We rarely stop there at the start of the trip as the urge to paddle is strong so soon after launching. Keep it in mind for your return.

This coast features some tiny little coves tucked behind rock outcrops, which you will find accessible thanks to the special qualities of the kayak. These sites give you the chance to observe marine life on the bottom, especially at low tide. In one such

Black oystercatchers

spot we caught sight of a graceful Kelp Crab (what a name!) clinging to a frond of seaweed. A scoop with a paddle and he was on our spray skirt. A feisty little fellow measuring 5–7 cm (2–3 in) across his smooth, pink carapace, he reared up in a threatening posture, waving his claws in the air to look as large and ferocious as possible. When we appeared sufficiently intimidated by his display, he scuttled sideways and vanished over the side.

A mile or so before you reach Nine Mile Point, an oyster farm backed by a sheer wall of granite appears. A couple of small Native Indian pictographs in red ochre are visible on this cliff, 3–4 m (10–15 feet) above the high-tide mark. These are good

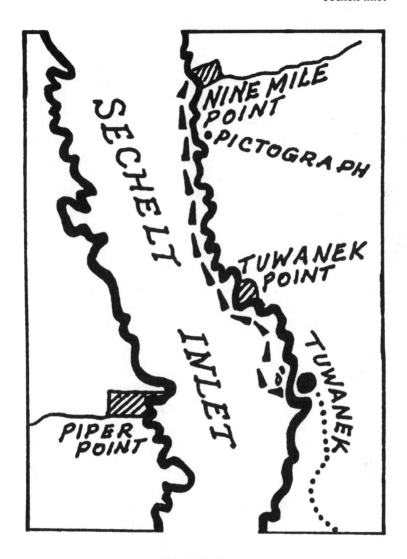

Nine Mile Point

examples of the many such pictographs scattered throughout the whole region which, we are told, may mean something as mundane as "Good fishing here" or "Watch for cougars."

Nine Mile Point has another small marine park with a great beach. By this time you may wish to stretch your legs a bit as there is no other suitable landing spot for some distance.

This is a great camping spot! In summer, families of mergansers hang out along this stretch of coast. The ruddy crest of the mother bird stands erect while she herds her little ones before her, seeking suitable cover until you finally pass. These birds band together to share the nurturing chores so occasionally you see prodigious numbers of young in a group.

Watch for eagles parked in their snags. Their acrobatic dives for prey are quite spectacular. Each foray over the water is accompanied by crows and gulls, harassing the eagles and hoping to cadge a share of the bounty.

The trip from Tuwanek to Nine Mile Point provides a full paddling experience. You may wish to simply explore this area a bit and then return the way you came, taking time to stop at Tuwanek Park.

TRIP TIME

4 hours for a leisurely paddle from Tuwanek to Nine Mile Point and back, with stops to rest and eat. If you choose to put in the water closer to town, you will need to add paddling time.

Should you wish to paddle east up Salmon Inlet, be aware that this can be a windy trip with few available landing spots. The 13-km (8-mi) paddle from here to Thornhill Creek takes about 3 hours.

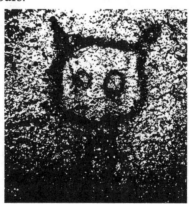

COMMON MERGANSER

Paddling along the coast on a warm day in early summer, you spot a large duck with a rust-coloured crest herding a flotilla of chicks ahead of her. Mergansers hatch large families, and you can often see a couple of harried females sharing the responsibility for their combined broods.

Mergansers are one of our most common year-round residents. The male has a beautiful green head like a mallard,

 *but its white body is larger, longer and slimmer than a mallard. Mergansers dive and pursue their prey under water, mainly small fishes or swimming insects they scoop up with their specialized bills.*

SECHELT INLET EXTENDED TRIPS

KUNECHIN POINT PROVINCIAL PARK

GETTING THERE

Launch from Porpoise Bay or the Tuwanek area as described in the Sechelt Inlet trips above.

CAUTIONS

The hazards here are related to winds. The daily winds will be at their worst at midday, so it is best to cross in the morning or late afternoon if possible. The mouth of Salmon Inlet is the windiest spot in the area, so expect confused seas and heavy chop if the winds are blowing. Assess the current weather and trends before deciding to cross.

Water from mountain streams is available in many of the parks on the inlet. Consume this water with caution, especially in the summer months when flows are minimal. If you must use it, treat with disinfectant or boil it first.

Black bears inhabit the hills around all these bodies of water. Allow them and other wildlife access to water by setting your

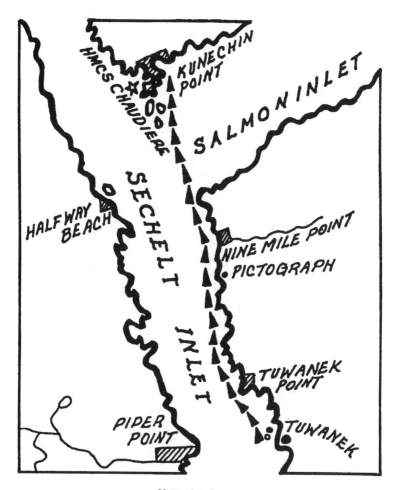

Kunechin Point

camp away from fresh water supplies. Do not leave garbage around the camps. Take it home with you or burn it thoroughly. Do not store food in your tent or in your kayak. A determined bear will stop at nothing to get at the goodies. If he wants it, let him have it. When hiking, carry a bell or knock rocks together to announce your presence.

THE TRIP

Follow the eastern shore of the Sechelt Inlet to the mouth of

Salmon Inlet. Directly across the mouth of Salmon Inlet, a couple of small islands stand in front of an irregular point with rocky shores. This is Kunechin Point and its associated islets.

In 1992 an artificial reef was created just off Kunechin Point with the sinking of the HMCS *Chaudiere*, a decommissioned war ship. Now the area is a very popular destination for divers, so you may see dive boats patiently tending their charges under the waves.

The confluence of the two inlets is especially good for fishing, which draws lots of seals to the area. The large number of summer visitors tends to drive the colonies off, but each spring they congregate here again to enjoy the bounty.

Kunechin Point Provincial Marine Park is, like all the parks in the inlet, largely undeveloped. Camping is welcomed here and sanitary facilities are provided. The water source is not reliable, as water is difficult to find and dries up entirely in the summer. Remember that these parks enforce a policy of garbage in, garbage out, so behave accordingly.

A weekend stay will give you time to explore the area further by paddling east up Salmon Inlet and north up Sechelt Inlet.

Entering Tzoonie Narrows, Narrows Inlet

The coast is rucked up with rock ridges, giving way to pocket beaches below a tree-covered upland. If you want to take a hike, be prepared to do some climbing.

TRIP TIME
About 3 hours from Tuwanek to Kunechin Point.

Alternate trip:
HALFWAY BEACH PROVINCIAL PARK

Follow the directions to Nine Mile Point as outlined in the Nine Mile Point trip. Cross to the western shore of the Sechelt Inlet heading slightly north and west. This course brings you to Halfway Islet with a broad bay and Halfway Beach behind. We think this is the nicest camping area on the inlet, a fine place to spend a weekend. A mountain stream runs through the camp, adding to the ambience. But remember that these waters are not potable.

In the spring, seals congregate in large numbers on the rocks around Halfway Island to take advantage of the great fishing in the area. By summer their numbers are reduced as human visitors begin using their space.

Half a mile south is Skaiakos Point—another park, but completely undeveloped at this writing. All in all you can visit five parks on this route, including Piper Point 3 km (2 mi) farther down the west side of the inlet.

Those same daily winds that make crossing the inlet a challenge can carry you effortlessly south like a sailboat. Be sure to wait for winds to moderate in the late afternoon if necessary.

Piper Point is almost directly across from Tuwanek, so you can make a final crossing to the east to get back at your starting point after a rigorous and varied weekend.

TRIP TIME
4 to 6 hours, depending on the route you take and your skills. A good weekend trip.

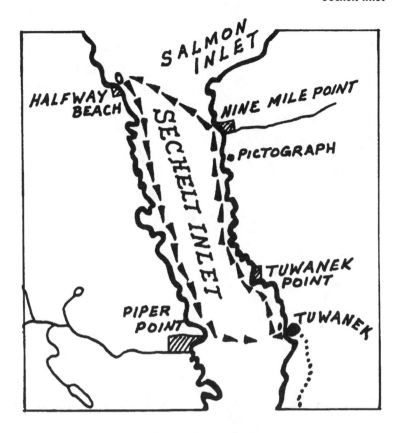

Halfway Beach Provincial Park

NARROWS INLET– TZOONIE NARROWS

GETTING THERE

Launch from the Tuwanek area as described in the Sechelt Inlet trips above.

CAUTIONS

You can encounter stiff winds on this trip, as in other trips in this area, especially between mid-morning and late afternoon. Wind and a brisk chop can be a problem at the mouth of Salmon Inlet, and landing sites are hard to find.

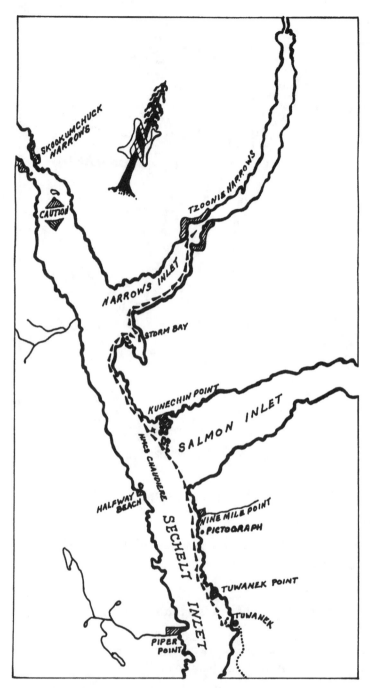

Narrows Inlet – Tzoonie Narrows

Sechelt Inlet

Skookumchuck Narrows Special Caution

The northwest end of the Sechelt Inlet constricts drastically where it joins Jervis Inlet, becoming the Skookumchuck Narrows. The entire tidal exchange between Jervis Inlet and Sechelt Inlet flows through this narrow channel, creating spectacular tide rips with standing waves, overfalls and whirlpools. The rapids can attain rates of 10–14 knots at spring tides with as much as 5 m (16 feet) of overfall. Whirlpools open suddenly and then disappear. Although whitewater paddlers love the place, it is only for the true adrenalin junkie and not recommended at all for touring kayaks. Reports abound of large motor vessels getting held in whirlpools, so imagine what awaits the hapless kayaker who gets in there at the wrong time. We once met a couple of young paddlers who entered the rapids with no knowledge of what they were getting into. One had his paddle ripped out of his hands by the current; by some miracle they both survived.

The rapids can be safely traversed by sea kayak at slack tide, but reference to the appropriate tide tables is essential before venturing onto the water.

THE TRIP

From the lower reaches of the inlet, paddle to Kunechin Point as described in the Kunechin Point trip (above). Continue north up the Sechelt Inlet to the mouth of Narrows Inlet. The shores are steep with a few tiny beaches. Sea urchins graze on the rock surface just below the water line, drawn by the occasional stand of bull kelp. Watch for the dark bulbs floating on the surface, the thick stem wandering behind and the long, graceful fronds undulating in the flow of the current.

Views of the coastal mountains up the inlet are quite wonderful from here. One spring day we paddled this trip through water that was smooth as glass, and a perfect image of the mountains, the sky and ourselves was reflected in the water. It was like paddling across a mirror, and gave us an eerie feeling of being suspended in space.

As you turn into the mouth of Narrows Inlet, take some time to explore Storm Bay, just to your right. In the 1960s this was a favourite spot for flower children to set up housekeeping, and some of the structures on shore reflect this past. Tree-lined shores, rocky cliffs and long shallows provide a tranquil resting spot before the next leg of your journey to Tzoonie Narrows.

Halfway up the inlet, the land pinches in at Tzoonie Narrows, creating a tidal current running about 3 knots at full flow. This is noticeable when you work against it and great fun when you go with it, so plan your day to ride the current if possible. Many sea creatures prefer places where the current flows so you will see lots of life in the water.

The public park runs along both sides of the narrows with the east side set up for camping. At this writing there is a privately owned campground about 1 km (.6 mi) south of the public park, which offers a hot tub on the shore, hot showers and a covered kitchen and eating area. The second commercial accommodation is a charming float house near the end of the inlet.

Continue along the east shore toward the head of the inlet. In one of our trips to this area we were drifting along about halfway between the narrows and the head of the inlet when we heard the roar of running water in the trees. Upon investigating, we found a beautiful glade of huge old trees festooned with moss, and two waterfalls cascaded down the mountainside behind them, filling the air with mist. A magical place indeed.

The Tzoonie River empties into the end of the inlet. At high tide we paddled upstream as far as we could. This was not very far at all as the river is narrow and filled with fallen trees and other obstructions, but it was an interesting exploration just the same. We went up far enough that turning around was a bit difficult with our long boats.

This inlet is ideal for family activities. It is well protected, there are beaches for kids and hikes up the surrounding hills. Transport by launch can be arranged from Sechelt.

TRIP TIME
7–8 hours from Tuwanek to Tzoonie. It is possible to do the trip in 2 days if you do a lot of paddling and not much messing around. Leave 3 days for a more enjoyable trip.

Halfmoon Bay

Northwest of Sechelt on Highway 101, the road winds along the coast through a wilder landscape in which forests begin to dominate the scene.

SARGEANT BAY

GETTING THERE

West of Sechelt, Highway 101 leaves the shoreline just before Sargeant Bay. Redrooffs Road veers off to the left about 6 km (3.6 mi) from Sechelt. This road is marked with one small sign only so watch carefully. Follow Redrooffs for 2 km (1.2 mi), watching for signs for Sargeant Bay Park Road. The road heads down to the shoreline on your left. Go 500 m (.3 mi) down this road and you are in a small park right on the water at the head of the bay. From the beach, the long fetch of the Strait of Georgia unfolds before you with the Trail Islands peeking out off the eastern point.

A cobble beach confronts you, but it gradually changes to

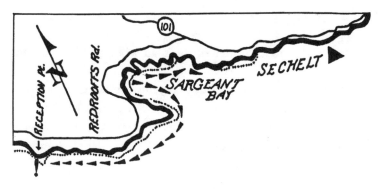

Sargeant Bay

sand. This is a great place for swimming or simply lazing in the sun. The sand then gives way to large boulders and rock cliffs on either side of the bay with homes and cottages nestled among them. The marsh behind the beach features pleasant, well-marked hiking trails through a wooded haven for birds and other wildlife. A local volunteer group has devoted itself to restoring the area, cleaning up the deadfall in the woods and freeing the water flow in the creek. This is a very popular spot for birdwatchers.

Launch your boat over a short stretch of beach, where the larger stones have been scraped away to form a path for easy entry to the water.

CAUTIONS

The southeasterly winds of winter howl into this little bay impeded only by the Trail Islands in front. The bay provides protection from westerlies, making this a spot to remember when the winds blow. Be aware that on leaving the protection of the western point, you will be subject to the full force of the weather on the open strait.

If you proceed west along the shore, you enter Welcome Passage between Merry Island and the mainland. This can be a most hazardous area when southerly or westerly winds are strengthened as they funnel through the pass. Winds in opposition to the tidal flow will increase the hazard.

Large numbers of commercial and recreational vessels of all descriptions use Welcome Passage, so be especially careful to know and follow the rules of the road when paddling in this area.

Keep a sharp eye out for the many huge boulders in the water off the western point of Sargeant Bay. A couple of times we scraped the bottoms of our kayaks passing over them. In rougher weather it would be advisable to paddle well offshore.

THE TRIP
Paddle out of the bay and around the rocky headland, and head west along the coast. It pays to dawdle here to watch for schools of small fish feeding among the boulders scattered offshore. Herons carefully pick their way through the rocks, checking out those same schools.

Once around the point you will follow a high escarpment with a cobble beach at its foot. The slopes are heavily wooded and birdsong is clearly audible throughout the afternoon. Swallows take swooping forays low over the water, snapping up bugs. Marbled Murrelets scoot off when approached, while a pair of Bald Eagles survey the area from the heights as their

Sargeant Bay

offspring fly from tree to tree below them. There is considerable human settlement on the top of the cliff but it is not visible from the water, giving you a sense of solitude.

Merry Island appears to the west, easily identified by the red and white lighthouse blinking on the nearest point.

We paddled to Reception Point with its light marking the eastern boundary of Welcome Passage before looking for a beach to rest on. The beaches are pretty rocky for a comfortable landing. Behind a high berm thrown up by the fierce winter winds, we found a little cove where we pulled in easily, a basin of sand with seaweed and crabs flourishing in the protection of the cobble shelf. A kingfisher, perched at the water's edge, darted off with that characteristic rattling call as we drew near.

TRIP TIME
3 hours for a leisurely paddle with plenty of time for lazing on the beach and taking pictures. There is no limit to the time you can spend exploring this area.

ALTERNATE TRIPS
The Sargeant Bay launch site puts you in the centre of a network of short trips. You can easily reach the Trail Islands to the east or Merry Island to the west for a nice day-long paddle.

The paddle up the eastern side of the bay offers a mix of steep rocks and pocket beaches. We took our two grandchildren on this trip and they were thrilled with the varied experiences open to them. It was an ideal setting to introduce them to paddling on their own—we could allow them to paddle around freely in the safety of this lovely bay.

leaves glowing yellow spotted green
twirl and spin carried on the wind
traveling traveling slowly down
a gust tumble twirls and a spin
finally to rest in a grave yard
of pilotless planes

HALFMOON BAY

Halfmoon Bay is a large, protected bay facing south. Its eastern curve is characterized by gentle sand or rock beaches with Redrooffs Road behind. Homes and cottages line this inviting shoreline.

The western side is much rockier but just as well populated. Winter winds pounding this coast have beat it back to the rock skeleton. The shore is wrinkled into many interesting little coves.

At the head of the bay sits the village of Halfmoon Bay, with a post office, a general store, a small craft shop and a public wharf. A local potter was busy at her wheel in the shop when we visited there. The general store was clearly set up to serve the boating public and fulfills this mandate admirably.

Looking south from the public wharf, South Thormanby Island looms off the point to your right across Welcome Passage, while Merry Island sits off the shore to your left. The Merry Island light station is just visible on the eastern shore of the island. This light station marks the entrance to Welcome Passage and its shoals, as well as reporting wind conditions to the Coast Guard.

Welcome Passage, a narrow strip of water with steep sides, separates the mainland from South Thormanby. Just off the western shore, at the entrance to the passage, a cluster of bare rocks rises out of the sea.

GETTING THERE

Drive northwest along Highway 101 and turn left at Redrooffs Road, about 6 km (3.6 mi) from the northwest edge of Sechelt. Redrooffs winds through rural settlements until it meets the shoreline and then follows the eastern shore of Halfmoon Bay.

If you miss the turnoff, don't despair. Redrooffs Road makes a loop and rejoins the highway just past the village. This approach is more visibly marked on the highway, with a sign indicating the turnoff and, parked opposite Redrooffs, a truck holding a sign that advertises the general store. Turn left.

We have used three launching sites on Redrooffs Road.

The first is the public wharf. Turn down Mintie Road, which is announced by another sign for the general store, and follow the road past the store to the public wharf.

The second is Welcome Beach, opposite Merry Island. Turn onto Redrooffs at the southern end, about 6 km (3.6 mi) from Sechelt, and follow it for about 7 km (4 mi). Watch for a street sign marking Welcome Beach Road and turn left, toward the water. There is a small public beach here, with limited parking space adjacent to it.

The third is Coopers Green, about 2 km (1.2 mi) farther along Redrooffs from Welcome Beach. You can see it from the road. It is a public recreation area with ample parking, outdoor bathrooms and a community hall. Take Fisherman's Road to the parking lot and launch from the beach.

If you prefer not to paddle the length of Halfmoon Bay on your way to the islands, follow the highway past Redrooffs Road to Brooks Road and turn toward the water. This road is the second turnoff to the left past Redrooffs and is marked with the city street sign only, so watch carefully. Drive to the end of the road, where you will find a turnaround with room to park several vehicles. This little bay is called Frenchman's Cove. The beach here is pretty rocky and the cove is open to the southeasterlies, so pick your day to use this site.

CAUTIONS

Southeast winds in the Strait of Georgia are often strongest along the Sunshine Coast. These winds are strengthened in Welcome Passage because they are funnelled between the cliffs lining the channel. Southeast waves will steepen on ebb currents through Welcome Passage, creating rough seas.

The tidal stream intensifies where the passage is narrowest,

Merry Island Lighthouse in background

east of Merry Island and northeast of South Thormanby. The
seas may be steepest and most confused off Lemberg Point and
east of Merry Island where the bottom depths are irregular and

where swells from the open gulf often enter at an angle to the wind and tidal stream.

One of the difficulties here is that Welcome Passage looks so benign. It is less than a mile across and seems to be well protected by islands, but this special configuration can create very hazardous waters. Check conditions before you cross and be prepared to wait out the weather on the island if necessary. There are public telephones on the beach at Buccaneer Bay and on the public wharf at Vaucroft Beach if you need them. Be sure you have a quarter!

MERRY ISLAND

Launch from Welcome Beach and paddle due south toward Merry Island, a crossing of just over a mile.

Merry Island is a particularly beautiful island with its rocky shores rising out of deep waters. A mixed forest covers the middle of the island and the shores are carpeted with many varieties of mosses in shades of green.

We were there one cool, damp day in December. The tide

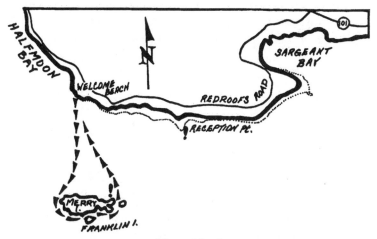

Merry Island

was at its highest so all the seals were fishing in the passes, poking their heads up to watch us. Harlequin Ducks scurried away as we rounded a corner. On the southern face of the island, large flocks of Bonaparte's Gulls squabbled and dove as they fed madly on a passing school of fish. The frenzy over, they sat in tranquil lines along floating logs awaiting the next meal.

Tiny Franklin Island nestles on the south side of Merry Island. This rocky outcrop is a bird sanctuary, and signs of nests are evident as you drift by the shores. In spring and summer when the birds are raising their young, you must give them a wide berth. Any interference can cause injury to the young. On the winter day that we visited, few birds were in residence and the rocks of Franklin Island were covered with lichen, glowing green to orange in the diffuse light.

The Merry Island light station occupies the southeastern tip of the island. Here is the quintessential lighthouse, a white tower with red trim and the beacon flashing its message of warning and safe haven. This is the only manned light station on the Sunshine Coast, and two families share round-the-clock weather reports and other duties.

The eastern end of the island has many shoals and would

be most interesting to explore in low tide, but for us the day was drawing to a close. As the rain began in earnest, we headed back to our vehicle with a strong desire to return again to Merry Island.

TRIP TIME

3 to 4 hours. Set aside a full afternoon to make the round trip at a leisurely pace.

JEDDAH POINT AND WELCOME PASSAGE

The trip to Jeddah Point is a good choice for the beginning paddler as it is shoreline paddling in a settled area.

Launch from the public wharf at Halfmoon Bay and paddle along the western shore of the bay. Human habitation blankets this coast, with a house on every headland and in each bay. Just before Welcome Passage, two long fingers of sea reach into the peninsula, Brooks Cove and Frenchman's Cove. A smattering of rock islets guards the entrance to these two coves and as you slip past them you are completely protected on all sides from wind and waves. Quiet tranquility prevails. The end of Frenchman's Cove enters Smuggler Cove Provincial Park. Various ducks and gulls cruise these quiet waters and the occasional seal watched as we slipped by.

As you poke your nose past these islands and round Jeddah Point, you will taste the mood of Welcome Passage. The cliffs concentrate the strength of wind and water, producing a powerful funnelling effect—a change you can feel strongly in the water.

The largest island here is a steep, bare rock with shoals at its base. We clambered out of our kayak and had lunch at the top. Seals fed in the passage while an oystercatcher sat on her nest on a rock shoal below us. A pair of young lovers paddled their dinghy to these rocks to enjoy each other in privacy.

Follow the cliffs along Welcome Passage and enjoy the variety of wildlife and splendid scenery open to you here.

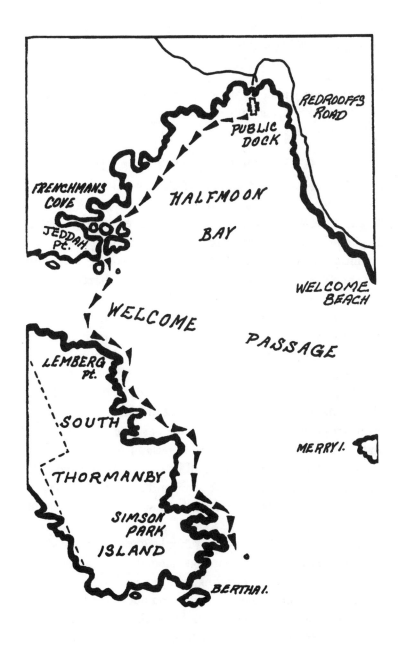

Jeddah Point–Welcome Passage–South Thormanby Island

The trip home is an easy paddle to the wharf, especially if tides and winds are with you.

TRIP TIME

2 hours if you paddle hard, but we recommend you take your time and make it a pleasant afternoon paddle, enjoying the flora and fauna of the area.

SOUTH THORMANBY ISLAND

Launch from the public wharf in Halfmoon Bay and paddle up the northwest side of the bay to Welcome Passage. Or take the Brooks Road–Frenchman's Cove alternative, turning left on Brooks Road from Highway 101 and following it to the water.

Either way, it is a good idea to evaluate conditions before you cross Welcome Passage, keeping in mind the hazards of this narrow waterway.

If all is well, head for Lemberg Point on the island. The eastern coast of South Thormanby is wrinkled into many small bays. The shore is rocky cliffs dropping into deep water with tiny beaches at the heads of the bays.

Simson Park covers the whole east side of the island and old logging trails lead down to most of the bays, making this a prime area to explore on foot. The area was once a working farm and the open fields are slowly being reclaimed by forest. They provide an excellent habitat for all kinds of songbirds, and the marshes teem with insect life. Dragonflies of many different colours and shapes were buzzing about when we were there in summer.

Low tide will bare masses of Purple Starfish grazing along the cliffs. Sea cucumbers are occasionally seen among the barnacles and seaweeds covering the steep walls.

We spent some time moving in and out of the bays along the coast, and as we rounded each headland we experienced increasing wind and wave action. It suddenly occurred to us that the southeasterly winds were freshening rapidly. We assessed

Welcome Beach   Keith Thirkell photo

the situation and saw that once we returned to Halfmoon Bay we would be at the mercy of the winds as we paddled back to the dock. So we chose to paddle across the bay to Welcome Beach and ride the wind home from there. It was a most exciting trip! We still aren't sure that this was an intelligent decision but it sure was fun.

If you head west through Welcome Passage and round Derby Point on the island, Buccaneer Bay opens out to your left. This wide bay lies between North and South Thormanby islands and offers the paddler many fine trips along its shores. See details about Buccaneer Bay in the Secret Cove chapter.

TRIP TIME
1 day. Count on at least 3 hours of paddling just to get there and back, then add the time you will need to enjoy hiking and leisurely exploration of the many bays.

SECRET COVE
Fingers of sea reach into the coast just north of Halfmoon Bay, creating a lacy effect on any map of the area. Marinas and homes line the shores of the largest of these, Secret Cove. Accessible

Secret Cove–Smuggler Cove–
Buccaneer Bay–Thormanby Islands

from the open sea through a narrow channel studded by islands and shoals, it offers a safe harbour in all weather.

Turnagain Island dominates the northwestern side of the cove. It looks like part of the mainland, and indeed it is separated only by a very narrow channel that dries at low tide—just right for a kayak to slip through.

The main channel out of the cove lies south from the public

wharf with Jack Tolmie Island bisecting it. Buoys mark the deep water for larger boats but the kayak can use any of the channels when the tide is high enough.

Outward from the cove and along the eastern shore, rocks rise out of the water, here gently, there more steeply. Smuggler Cove Marine Park encompasses the majority of this coastline, including Smuggler Cove itself. One of the most popular anchorages on the coast, it is used extensively by all kinds of boaters, especially in the summer. The pattern of Secret Cove is repeated here on a smaller scale, and you slip past Isle Capri through a narrow passage into a totally protected cove. A couple of private summer cottages perch on the rocks, throwbacks to the time before the park was created. The public is welcome to use the amenities here without encroaching on the private areas.

Welcome Passage is at its narrowest between Grant Island, at the top of the point, and South Thormanby Island. Across the Passage and around Derby Point, you enter Buccaneer Bay. The shoals of Tattenham Ledge stretch north from the point and provide a rich hunting ground for seals and seabirds of all kinds. Buccaneer Bay sits between North and South Thormanby islands with the Surrey Islands marching along the western coast of South Thormanby. At the end of the bay, long sand flats culminate in Gill Beach, said to be the most beautiful beach on the Sunshine Coast. There is a small .4-ha (1-acre) provincial park at Grassy Point on the southern tip of North Thormanby.

Sunset over Texada Island   Keith Thirkell photo

North Thormanby looks like one huge sand dune thrown up by the southeasterlies that howl down the strait in winter. On its southeastern aspect, the cliffs of sand reveal their stratas to the world as the sand slides into the water, creating long, shallow sand flats. The trees bristle in a brush cut of green along the top of the cliff. How the birds love these rich waters, renewed by tides and winds, and warmed by sand and sun.

GETTING THERE

Follow Highway 101 north past the turnoff to Halfmoon Bay. Watch for signs for Secret Cove. At this point, the highway starts a long, slow climb. The road veers off to the left partway up the hill.

Less than 1 km (.6 mi) along this road, turn left at Secret Cove Road, marked by a sign. This short road carries you down the hill to the public wharf at the end. We always drive right down to the beginning of the wharf, unload and then take the vehicle back up the road to park it. The road is steep, so chock your wheels with a rock.

CAUTIONS

Welcome Channel and its special features figure largely in the hazards of any trip out of Secret Cove. The geography of the passage concentrates the effect of winds and tidal currents. Remember also the corner phenomenon—all weather conditions are intensified around a headland.

Marine traffic is heavy in Welcome Passage so keep the rules of the road in mind when crossing here.

We learned the hard way about the hazards associated with the splendid sand beaches found on Thormanby Island. The tide retreats with amazing speed over long, slow slopes and those inviting sand flats can turn into a trap—marooning you far from the water. Walking in this stuff is no fun at the best of times and a real drag under a load.

Awareness of the prevailing westerlies and southeasterlies is critical when travelling the exposed coasts of the islands and crossing Welcome Passage.

SMUGGLER COVE

Launch from the public wharf at the foot of Secret Cove Road, paddle out of the cove past Jack Tolmie Island and head south down the coast. To the west you see the long fetch of Malaspina Strait with Texada Island in the distance. Drift along the shoreline examining the sea life in the shallows, and get ashore on the rocky beaches that occur from time to time.

Watch for the plaque marking the entrance to Smuggler Cove to your left as you round Isle Capri and slip through into the cove. A combination of rock faces and sand flats greets you here. Sea cucumbers lie on the submerged rocks, and ducks and geese cruise the calm surface of the water.

As the marine park covers a large area, for a change of pace leave your kayak and enjoy the walking trails that meander through the park.

When you have had your fill of the cove, return to Welcome Passage and continue east toward Halfmoon Bay. Now the nature of the water will change as the seas here are constantly moving with winds and tides. We saw a river otter swimming along the water's edge, almost perfectly camouflaged by the play of light and dark where the land and water meet. Landing spots are small and apt to be rocky, but they afford a chance to enjoy some solitude.

TRIP TIME

At least 3 hours. The paddle from Secret Cove to Smuggler Cove, a distance of about 2 km (1.2 mi), takes 30 minutes. Spend a pleasant hour or two exploring the cove and Welcome Passage before returning to Secret Cove—an excellent afternoon on the water.

BUCCANEER BAY

Launch from the public wharf at the foot of Secret Cove Road and paddle out of the cove into Malaspina Strait. Looking south across Welcome Passage, you will see Derby Point, the northernmost tip of South Thormanby Island, ahead of you. This is a distance of about 2.4 km (1.5 mi), and time available and weather conditions will dictate your route to this point. You can head straight out for the point, which will take you across a long stretch of open water and give you that wonderful sense of being alone in a vast expanse in the relative safety of a busy waterway. Alternatively, you can follow the contour of the coast and explore all the way. Crossing Welcome Passage with caution, you will pass through the shoals of Tattenham Ledge, then round the point into Buccaneer Bay. There is a small kelp forest just around the point where marine life abounds. Seals and seabirds patrol the area searching for lunch.

South along the western shore of South Thormanby you will next encounter the Surrey Islands. The gnarled, twisted shapes of windswept trees against rocks and sea are evocative of the serenity and beauty of a Japanese block print. These shores are home to a variety of sea life.

Evening red, morning grey
Sets the traveller on his way;
Evening grey, morning red
Brings down rain upon his head.

Continuing south, round Wolf Point—and there before you is Gill Beach. You leave the rocks behind and the sand flats stretch ahead. Carpets of emerald green sea grass offer cover for crabs of all kinds and the tide-washed sand flats are home to millions of clams. (We do not recommend digging clams here. There are too many humans using the bay.) The shore just above Gill Beach is privately owned and the residents are not at all keen to share "their" beach with strangers, so do not impose on their property. As you paddle across the bay along the spit, the settlement ends and boaters of all kinds can enjoy the warm sands and splendid swimming that this area offers. There is a narrow channel between the two islands but it is dry most of the time. On occasion we have slipped through at the highest tide, and we've also portaged to the outside shore to play in the surf.

The western shore of North Thormanby offers marked contrast to its counterpart across the bay. This shore is sandy and shallow with gentle wooded slopes rising behind. At Grassy Point on the southern tip of the island is a small provincial park where you can explore or just rest.

At the northern end of North Thormanby you will find Vaucroft Beach and Oaks Point with a public wharf. Please respect the privacy of people living in the settlement of summer cottages here. You can hike across the island to Epsom Point if you wish. This is a lengthy walk, so give yourself plenty of time. You can also walk around the northern end of the island on the beach for as far as you like.

It is a 3-km (2-mi) paddle over open water if you head directly back to Secret Cove from Oaks Point. Given favourable weather conditions, this is a most enjoyable paddle with the coastal mountains rising ahead of you as you head for home.

TRIP TIME

1 day. It will take 3 hours of paddling to get there and back, and you'll find a lot of things to do and see on the way.

NORTH THORMANBY ISLAND

Launch from the public wharf at the foot of Secret Cove Road, then leave the cove and head for Oaks Point on North Thormanby. Remember the funnelling and channelling effects that prevail in Welcome Passage. Winds and waves can be severe here. You will be travelling on the exposed coasts of the island so be aware of the prevailing winds that come from the west and the southeast. The summer westerlies usually wane in the late afternoon, so you may want to wait them out if the trip back from Oaks Point to Secret Cove seems too threatening.

Continue west around the island from Oaks Point. You will be paddling over sand flats with high stratified sand cliffs behind. The sea bottom is easily visible from your kayak as you move across these rich feeding grounds. Schools of small fish appear from time to time and crabs lurk in the sea grass. Because the beaches on the western side of the island are uninhabited by humans, they are frequented by all kinds of shorebirds, and

BONAPARTE'S GULL

Small and graceful, the Bonaparte's Gull floats placidly on the sea or scurries busily along the line of the tide as it ebbs. In summer the male has a coal black head and red feet, while the winter plumage is white except for grey across the wings and

back and a grey smudge behind the eye. The long triangle of white found on the leading edge of the wing with black edges at the wingtip distinguish this gull from the very similar Franklin's Gull.

seals cruise the warm, shallow water. There are many places to land and eat, explore or stretch your legs. The tide moves in and out quickly over such shallow ground and these sand flats are no fun to carry a kayak across, so watch the tidal movements.

Continue paddling along this coast until you reach Grassy Point at the southern end of the island. The cliffs and rock formations at Grassy Point are particularly impressive. If the tides are high when you reach this spot, you can portage across the spit and return to your starting point by paddling north through Buccaneer Bay. Be sure to reconnoitre before you commit yourself to the portage—it can be a long haul if the tide is low. Otherwise, return the way you came. The crossing from Epsom Point to Secret Cove is a distance of 5 km (3 mi) and takes about an hour of paddling with no stops.

TRIP TIME
At least 3 hours. It will take 1 ¾ hours to paddle to the bay and return to Secret Cove, but take an afternoon to really enjoy everything this trip has to offer. A full day of paddling and walking is available here.

North Thormanby sand flats   Keith Thirkell photo

JEDEDIAH ISLAND EXTENDED TRIP

Jedediah Island is the Sunshine Coast's newest marine park. The largest island in an archipelago marching along the eastern shore of Lasqueti Island, it nestles in Sabine Channel across from Texada Island. This 25-ha (64-acre) island has been a summer retreat and a working homestead since it was first settled early in the century. The last tenants worked the farm until the early 1980s, leaving evidence of their endless toil all over the island. A lovely old farmhouse overlooks the lagoon in Home Bay. The barn and other outbuildings, all constructed of native trees, border the orchard. Farmyard, orchard and wide pastures are cradled in a bowl of granite.

Around the shore, steep cliffs soar out of the water to face the sea. On every side long bays, most of which dry at low tide, punch through to the interior. Home Bay opens off Sabine Channel on the southeast side of the island, while Long Bay and Deep Bay—yes it is deep and therefore a favourite of boaters—are tucked in on the northwestern side.

Rabbit Island, Circle Island, Bull Island, Paul Island, Jervis Island and their attendant islets and shoals make up the rest of this "String of Pearls" with Jedediah as the central gem. The wide swath of Bull Passage swings past Jervis Island to exit onto the Strait of Georgia between Lasqueti and Bull Island. Bull Passage squeezes between the cliffs of Jedediah and Bull Island.

Eagles sit in dignified solitude on snags while groups of sea ducks swarm below. Ospreys teach their young hunting skills while river otters dive and roll. All of them take nourishment from the richness of the sea. This is a paradise for the paddler.

GETTING THERE

Jedediah Island can be reached from any of the launch sites that take you to Thormanby, as this will be your first stop on the trip. The public wharf at the end of Secret Cove Road is the best choice as it offers protected water in any weather. The wharf is crowded in summer and parking is limited. Halfmoon Bay and

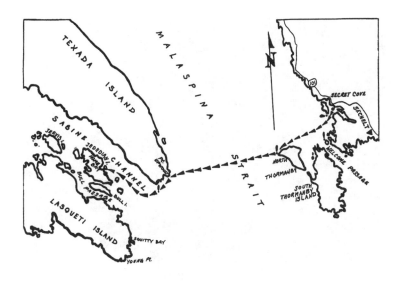

Jedediah Island

the beach in Frenchman's Cove are other possibilities. French-man's Cove (at the end of Brooks Road) has parking and lies close to the water, but the beach is rocky, strewn with logs, muddy at low tide and open to southeast winds. So take your pick.

CAUTIONS
The trip to Jedediah involves crossing some of the most danger-ous and unpredictable waters along the Sunshine Coast. The weather is particularly changeable in winter, so it is probably best to choose another destination at that time of year. In summer, make your crossing in the early morning or late afternoon or evening to avoid the daily winds. Choose the hours around slack tide for the Thormanby–Texada leg of the trip if possible.

An examination of the chart will show you the problems—a long fetch to the south and the intersection of Welcome Passage, Malaspina Strait, Sabine Channel and the Strait of Georgia. Wind and tides are subject to funnelling and channelling effects between Thormanby Island and the mainland in Welcome

Jedediah Island

Passage, in Sabine Channel and up Malaspina Strait. The undulating seabed through the area alters the pattern of the waves, usually for the worse.

Corner winds will increase the intensity of the weather on all headlands, particularly Epsom Point on Thormanby and the southern tips of Texada and Lasqueti Islands.

The south ends of the islands are subject to the full fetch of the Strait of Georgia to the southeast, so wave heights will be at their maximum here. Westerlies will build through the channels, creating confusing seas over the area.

These channels are also major shipping lanes for all manner of commercial and recreational vessels moving between Vancouver and Powell River, Campbell River and beyond. Expect to see lots of tugs moving through Malaspina Strait, Sabine Channel and Welcome Passage. Obey the rules of the road and stay out of their way.

There is no water on Jedediah Island. Make sure you have sufficient before you set out. If you must get water, find a shallow bay on Texada Island directly across from Circle Island.

A stream hurtles off the slope here. Treat the water before drinking it.

THE TRIP

Choose your launch site according to the best conditions at the time of launch, while keeping in mind possible conditions on your return. Make your way to Epsom Point on the western tip of North Thormanby. Now is the time for a thoughtful assessment of the conditions and your skills. Look both ways before you cross, as your mother used to caution you. Everything out there is probably bigger and faster than you, so plan accordingly.

Head for Point Upwood on the southern shore of Texada Island. There is an old trailer on a point in this area that serves as a marker for the crossing. If you have a compass, the bearing is 260 degrees. This bearing will put you in the vicinity of some small protected bays around Point Upwood at the end of an 8-km (5-mi) crossing. Grab some rest and reassess your situation. Camping is possible here if you cannot return safely.

Continue around the tip of Texada and head west diagonally across Sabine Channel, again with due caution for winds and traffic.

Jedediah Island

Jedediah Island

Huge sentinels of bare granite heave out of the sea at the start of the island chain, shielding the bays of Jedediah from the worst of the south winds. Cormorants rest on the shoals, wings hung out to dry. Seals roll languorously in the passes, watching warily as you slip by. Moving along the eastern shore of Jedediah you encounter a deep bay with a rock beach, another small wrinkle with lots of drift logs piled on the shore, and finally the narrow opening into Home Bay. This little defile is difficult to see until you are right on top of it! If you arrive at low tide the lagoon will be dry. We often land on that first rock beach, walk through to the lagoon, stake out a campsite, then go for a paddle until the water returns.

Level grassy areas under lowering trees behind a beach of soft, white sand make an ideal campsite in Home Bay. From the beach you look across the lagoon to the quaint little farmhouse perched on a knoll. The only pit toilets on the island at this time are tucked in the woods behind the beach. As the whole island is a park, you can camp in any of the bays around the perimeter.

One evening while we prepared supper, we spotted a family of Osprey circling our bay. One magnificent bird began a hovering action some hundred feet above the shallow water, then quickly plunged downward. It struck the water, made a quick recovery and up it went, carrying a small fish in its talons. One of the smaller birds hit the water and came up empty, having missed its target. Another strike and another miss. We agreed that it was the youngsters who were missing their targets, with the parent bird doing the teaching. Throughout the meal we held front row seats to a spectacular display of aerial acrobatics.

One of the joys of Jedediah is taking a late-night paddle in the lagoon. The luxurious bioluminescence creates a world of flashing comets and sparkling stars beneath your kayak. The myriad small creatures of the shallows excite an eerie green glow as they scoot out of harm's way.

If you are like us, moving camp constantly is not your idea of a good time. We usually set up camp in Home Bay and explore the islands from there.

Take time to walk across the island through woods and pastures. Springtime in that pasture is an orgy of wildflowers.

An old horse lives out his years here. A friendly fellow, he expects at least a pat or two even if nothing edible is offered. Sheep graze the flats, but they are wary and keep their distance. We suspect they augment the winter larder of many a local neighbour. You'll see goats on the cliffs as well. We are told they are descendants of animals left by the early explorers of the coast, who brought them as an emergency food supply.

Head south from Home Bay to check out the islets there. We found a precarious little haulout on the eastern side of one of these huge mounds and clambered up to the top. There it was, the whole of the Strait of Georgia laid out before us.

Little Bull Channel leads you between Jedediah and Bull Island. The steep walls of the channel give you a great opportunity to see the intertidal life at low tide. Tidal currents run up to 3 knots so you'll work if the tide is against you and soar effortlessly if it's with you. Moving water causes all life to proliferate, so look for seals, birds and undersea life in Little Bull Channel.

The shoals east of Jervis are home to a large seal colony. Pigeon Guillemots hide on ledges on the sheer cliffs nearby. The islets west of Jervis are a pleasure to explore. The southernmost islet of this group is made of sandstone which has been sculpted by wind and water into undulating waves of stone topped by a fringe of gnarled trees.

A trip around the southern tip of Lasqueti Island is a must if weather permits. The windswept shores give mute testimony to the power of the weather hurtling up the full fetch of the Strait.

Squitty Bay is a thoroughly picturesque little spot, a haven from those fierce winds off the Strait. There is a well with fresh water here, also a public wharf and some nice walking trails. A nice place to stop a while.

TRIP TIME

At least 2 days. Paddling from the mainland to Jedediah in

ideal conditions takes at least 3 hours, and realistically you should give yourself a day to get there and a day to get back. Enjoy as many days as you can spare to get the full flavour of this lovely place. We have often had to spend a day in camp due to inclement weather so give yourself plenty of time to get back.

Fish leap, existing but a moment free of the sea.
Just visible a snow capped mountain
stands silent.
Purples, blues and their transparent hues drop like a
stage curtain.
A slow rising moon glowing yellow,
yellow-white to white sends ripples of delight to
dance with the fish.

Pender Harbour

Pender Harbour

As you proceed north along Highway 101 past Halfmoon Bay, signs of human civilization become sparse. What settlement there is hugs the coast, leaving the highway to wind through forests and brush. Watch for signs indicating Pender Harbour.

On the map, Pender Harbour is a heavily indented coastal inlet protected from the open water of Malaspina Strait by the islands guarding the entrance and the large mass of Francis Peninsula.

The peninsula is very nearly an island, being connected to the mainland by a narrow strip of land, Bargain Narrows, that only dries at low tide. A short bridge spans the flats here. The bays flanking the bridge, Bargain Bay to the south and Gerrans Bay to the north, are both filled with shoals and gently sloping mud flats. The main body of the peninsula spreads out to cover the mouth of the harbour almost completely.

More and more people are settling here as they discover this beautiful spot. There are many homes along the road onto Francis Peninsula, which follows the coast to the west. The road comes to an end just past the harbour limit, and past this point, the seaward side of the peninsula is largely uninhabited. Signs of settlement are more widespread to the east. The landscape is quite mountainous through this whole region, and the road approaches the water's edge occasionally, but only in areas with long sand flats in front of them.

The village of Madeira Park is the largest town in the area. A shopping mall with a supermarket, a pharmacy, a restaurant, a liquor store, a gift shop and several hairdressers, is the centre of town. A little fast food joint serves coffee and burgers, chips and pop in the summer season. The school and a plenitude of marinas are among the other amenities. Down past the school at the edge of the water is the public wharf. The park nearby is home to a little art gallery that shows the work of local artists.

From the wharf, you can look out over Pender Harbour. Garden Peninsula is just across the harbour with Garden Bay behind. The Garden Bay Marine Park is a feature of this bay.

The other side of Garden Peninsula is Hospital Bay, named for the hospital that once occupied that shore. St. Mary's Hospital, now in Sechelt, served the area from the water for years before the road was built along the Sunshine Coast. The large white building still overlooks the bay, and houses a restaurant, inn and performance space.

Pender Harbour is a long one, reaching westward toward Malaspina Strait with many islets of varying sizes sprinkled through it. The shoreline is covered with dwellings and considerable construction is going on.

These waters are protected from all winds as the entrance to the harbour is dotted with islands—first the Skardon Islands, mostly bare rocks sitting in the middle of the channel, then Williams Island and Charles Island at the mouth of the harbour.

Irvines Landing lies on the northern shore of the harbour just before it opens out into the strait. The only public buildings in this community are the pub and the marina nearby.

As you move out of the harbour limits, you reach more islands. Martin and Pearson islands loom large before you and the little Hodgson Islands show on the horizon behind them.

Pender Harbour   Keith Thirkell photo

The Hodgsons are small islets of rock sitting just before the entrance to Agamemnon Channel. The rock is topped by a few small trees and a profusion of grasses, mosses and lichen interspersed with sedums and wildflowers.

GETTING THERE

Proceed northwest on Highway 101 from Langdale, through Gibsons and Sechelt, and watch for signs indicating Pender Harbour. Turn left onto Madeira Park Road and into town. The public wharf is on the shore beside the private marina. This seems to be the best bet for launching in the area.

We attempted to find a launch site on Francis Peninsula, but the mud flats were so extensive we were reluctant to try any promising launch sites. We thought we might return to find that we could not get back to our car.

Irvines Landing provides another good jumping-off place to explore this area. It also has the advantage of allowing more paddling time beyond the harbour limits. From Highway 101, take the turnoff for Garden Bay (Garden Bay Road) and proceed to Irvines Landing. There is a veritable maze of roadways

HARLEQUIN DUCK

Another denizen of the rocky headlands and islets of the BC coast, the Harlequin Duck dives for chitons, snails and crabs where currents have created surges. The male, a handsome fellow, is a slate blue with chestnut flanks and bold white markings outlined in black on the head and wings. The female and nonbreeding male are dark, and each has two or three white patches on its head.

These ducks are more solitary than goldeneyes and buffleheads but are occasionally seen in the company of scoters. Watch for them in small groups where water rushes around boulders and partly submerged ledges off rocky shores.

through this area serving the many homes along the shoreline and a dearth of signs to point you in the right direction. Generally, bear right as you drive, until you reach Irvines Landing. The wharf here does not have the familiar red paint on the railings, as our government has sold it to the marina. Check with them before launching.

CAUTIONS

Within the harbour limits the only hazard is other boats, of which there are lots and lots. Most boaters are thoughtful and cautious, but be on the lookout for the occasional idiot who can threaten your well-being.

As with most trips, the wind is the major hazard you will face when you paddle in Pender Harbour. For example, southeast gales cause gusty winds in the lee of coastal mountains, which affects this area.

On leaving the harbour you will find long fetches to the west and the south. These are also the directions of the prevailing winds on the coast, so proceed with caution. We have rarely been in this area when there has not been at least some wind on the strait, and there is often a 1-m (2- to 3-foot) chop beyond the lee of the islands.

On the trip to the Hodgson Islands, you are protected from westerlies by the islands themselves but subject to the southeasterlies, especially as you cross the mouth of Agamemnon Channel.

If you choose to explore Agamemnon Channel, the funnelling effect of its narrow shape will augment any south wind in the lower reaches of the channel. Outflow winds curling off the high cliffs will create lee effects—confused seas and gusty winds—against the shoreline here.

We must caution you again about the extensive mud flats around Francis Peninsula. When the tide recedes from these, it moves out very quickly over shallow areas. This stuff is almost impossible to walk over, especially with a kayak in tow. It's not a life-threatening condition, but we can tell you that after a short time slogging yourself and your kayak through this, you might wish you were dead.

THE HODGSON ISLANDS

Mah-kwee-lay-la, Kwakiutl for "it looks close but it seems to move away as you approach it," describes perfectly our experience on our trip to the Hodgson Islands. We emerged from the shelter of the harbour and there they were, these neat-looking islands just a short distance west of us. But they seemed to move away as we paddled toward them. That day was very clear and sunny, with a high-pressure system that typically produces this effect. When we look at these islets now we realize that they are, in fact, pretty close to shore, but to a beginning paddler they seem a long way out.

Launch from Madeira Park or Irvines Landing and head out of the harbour. The Hodgson Islands are the farthest group of islands you will see to the west, and the crossing is a nice paddle over open water. The islands are primarily bare rock with a very few small trees on the largest.

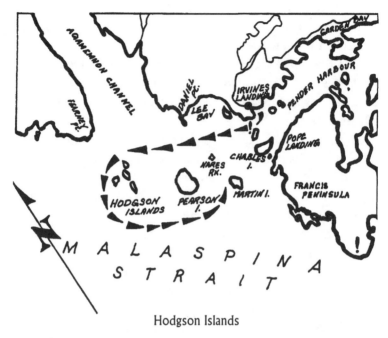

Hodgson Islands

The two largest islands are connected at low tide by a rock and gravel spit. We were able to land on this beach and climb to the top to view the whole area. It was a lovely spring day, and wildflowers grew everywhere. Large numbers of orchidlike yellow flowers nestled in most of the nooks and crannies in the rock. Tiny hot pink blooms sparkled across a low creeper.

Seals rested on the most westerly island, taking to the sea when they detected our presence. We watched them fishing in the waters around us while we ate our lunch.

On returning, we paddled around Pearson and Martin islands. There was much seaweed growing off these islands, fernlike fronds waving in the currents.

If you can plan your trip to follow the tides, you will minimize the work of paddling and maximize the distance you can go. The up-inlet winds of afternoon also can help to move you on your way.

Pender Harbour   Keith Thirkell photo

TRIP TIME

2 ½ to 3 hours minimum. It takes 30 minutes to paddle from the wharf at Madeira Park to the mouth of the harbour. Add another 30 minutes to get to the islets, more time to get around the larger islands, and 30 minutes more to return.

FRANCIS PENINSULA

We launched at Irvines Landing and proceeded south across the harbour and around the Peninsula. Williams and Charles islands offered some interesting shoreline to examine closely on the way.

Where Francis Peninsula Road ends, the houses stop and you feel alone in the wilderness. At present this is private, undeveloped land, so govern yourself accordingly. As we rounded Moore Point, the small beach in Francis Bay beckoned.

We climbed the rock cliff and settled down on the top of the ridge to eat lunch. At the beginning of our lunch we commented on the apparent lack of wildlife. We didn't even hear much in the way of birdsong. On this occasion we spent some extended time sitting there, and we found to our delight that this decision

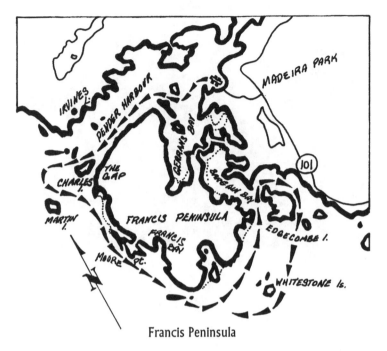

Francis Peninsula

paid great dividends. A ground squirrel darted out of the under-
brush, screeched to a halt on encountering us, and disappeared
in a flash. A pair of River Otters appeared at the edge of the
water, so well camouflaged in the ripples that we could just see
them, and then swam out in a line across the bay. High-pitched
cries filled the air. What was it? It didn't sound like any bird we
had ever heard. Turned out it was the otters whistling to one
another as they cavorted around the bay. A truly delightful
experience, and one that taught us the value of sitting quietly
in one place.

Continue around the peninsula to the mouth of Bargain
Bay. There is lots to explore here—Bargain Bay itself, Edge-
combe Island and the Whitestone Islands. The rocky islets
sprinkled around the area provide haulouts for seals and hunting
grounds for the seabirds that frequent the coast. Poke around to
your heart's content before retracing your route to your car.

TRIP TIME
At least 2 to 3 hours for the paddling. This is another trip that can be as long or as short as you wish.

NELSON ISLAND AND BLIND BAY
EXTENDED TRIP

Heading northwest from Pender Harbour you will cross Agamemnon Channel to Fearney Point on Nelson Island. This island is an enormous wedge of land tucked into the start of Jervis Inlet, and stretching from Malaspina Strait to the Skookumchuck Narrows. Like so much of the coast, the island is wrinkled into numerous bays and points with lots of mud flats, islets and shoals to enchant the paddler.

The shoreline offers up many artifacts from the past. Quarry Bay, for example, still has the remnants of an old quarry. Many of the wonderful old stone buildings of the Lower Mainland drew materials from this site, among them the lions on the steps of the Vancouver Art Gallery.

Over the past decades, the colourful characters of the coast found Nelson Island a refuge from the hurly burly of life, and built homesteads, boats and hideaways along the shores. Look for the remains of many an old farm in various stages of disrepair. The area continues to attract offbeat people and lovers of solitude. Cape Cockburn, the most westerly point of the island, was just such a getaway for Harry Roberts of the original Roberts Creek family. The site now belongs to BC Hydro and is the subject of intense lobbying by locals who wish to keep it as a park. Let's hope they are successful!

Around the point heading west, you will find myriad inlets, islands and islets on this fascinating shoreline. Blind Bay separates Nelson Island from its smaller neighbour, Hardy Island. It opens onto Jervis Inlet at the end, through Telescope Passage.

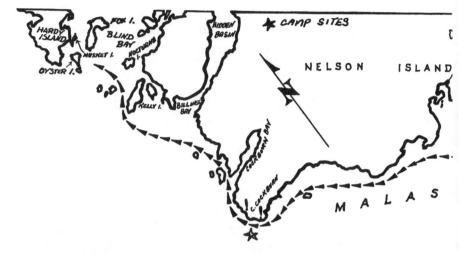

CAUTIONS

The south face of the island is subject to the full force of southeast winds coming up the strait. Look for corner winds around Cape Cockburn and lee effects all along the way. We have seldom been in this area when it has not been windy.

Malaspina Strait is a shipping lane leading to and from Powell River. Expect lots of tugs pulling booms, and various other commercial and recreational vessels, in the strait. As you will be following the shore, this traffic should not be of much concern.

THE TRIP

Enter the water at the Madeira Park wharf or Irvines Landing. Paddle out of Pender Harbour and head west to Agamemnon Channel.

Cross Agamemnon Channel to Fearney Point on Nelson Island and head west along the coast. The shoreline is much indented with little bays and points, and beaches and mud flats reach out into the sea. Quarry Bay, the first major bay, is worth looking at closely. The remains of old structures are underfoot while the rock cuts tell the story of the methods used to quarry this stone. At the head of the eastern finger of the bay, a stream

runs down to the long mud flat. There is a nice hiking trail here that takes you up to Little Quarry Lake, definitely worth the time and effort.

After rounding Cape Cockburn, you turn west. Look for Cockburn Bay cutting into the island on the north side of the cape. Long and narrow, it dries at low tide but is an ideal spot to explore when you are in a small kayak.

Moving along through the rock gardens of the coast, watch for the opening to Hidden Basin. Follow a shallow defile almost half a mile long into a lagoon of deeper water, a safe haven indeed in any kind of weather. From Ballet Bay at the end of the lagoon, find another hiking trail leading into Blind Bay, a good thing to remember if the weather on the strait is dangerous.

Farther north, Blind Bay opens before you, dividing Hardy Island from its larger neighbour. Here too there are lots of little bays, islands and islets, a pleasure to dawdle through like the birds of the area are wont to do.

Tiny Musket Island nestles up against the southeastern face of Hardy Island just beyond Malaspina Strait. This is another marine park which offers good camping opportunities.

Telescope Passage at the northern end of Blind Bay lives up

to its name, funnelling the waters of the bay into Jervis Inlet. Lots of rocks litter this alleyway to the Inlet, making it treacherous for larger boats but just fine for the little kayak.

You can return the way you came or take the long route around Nelson Island, down Agamemnon Channel and back to Pender Harbour. Or stay over on Nelson Island. There is another camping spot on the north end of the island, on a beach behind the light marking Agnew Passage, which runs between the tip of Nelson Island and Captain Island.

TRIP TIME

At least 2 days to Blind Bay and back. We know paddlers who have done this trip as a day trip, but they didn't have any time to linger and enjoy the spot.

At least 3 days for the trip around Nelson Island.

SURFBIRDS AND BLACK TURNSTONES

Rocky islets up and down the coast are home to mixed flocks of Surfbirds and Black Turnstones. Both birds belong to the sandpiper family, whose members have long legs, rotund bodies and sharp beaks. Surfbirds are mottled brown or black while the turnstone is dusky black above with a white belly.

These birds rummage through the flora and fauna in the

intertidal zone in search of crabs, beach hoppers and sand fleas. Friendly little creatures, they will tolerate you right next to them if you are calm and unhurried. The flock flies off in perfect unison, with the characteristic white markings on the wings and tails flashing in the sun.

Jervis Inlet

Jervis Inlet snakes its way inland off Malaspina Strait north of Hardy Island and Nelson Island, bisecting the upper and lower coast. Long, narrow and very deep, it zigzags north between the coastal mountains for 80 km (50 mi). Bounded on every side by mile-high mountains, Jervis is the deepest of BC's many inlets. It is an eerie feeling to paddle along knowing that there is some 900 m (3000 feet) of water under your boat.

The inlet was home to thriving villages of the Sechelt Indians 300 years ago, before their numbers were devastated by disease and despair. Miraculously, numerous pictographs survive the centuries on stone faces up and down the inlet. European place names now dominate these traditional lands, but the local First Nations and their cultural traditions have persisted.

Moving inland from Malaspina Strait, St. Vincent Bay and Hotham Sound open to the north opposite the north end of Nelson Island. Hotham Sound is a particularly gentle place. For some reason it is relatively free from the local winds that buffet other inlets. We can't remember ever being there when it was windy, although we know it must happen, especially on the east side of the sound. The mountain tarn, Freil Lake, pours over the cliffs to the quiet waters far below, a familiar landmark for those riding the ferry out of Earls Cove.

The Skookumchuck Narrows runs southeast from here.

Egmont wanders along the shore of the Narrows at the start of the Sechelt Rapids. This amazing tidal rapid can reach epic proportions on big spring tides with huge whirlpools and towering overfalls. Visitors from around the world hike in to watch the rapids in action. Whitewater paddlers rejoice in the challenge and scuba divers delight in the prolific life through the rapids.

As you head north, Prince of Wales Reach, Princess Royal Reach and finally Queens Reach carry you to the end of the inlet.

About 10 km (6 mi) from that end, a deep cleft opens to the north. Bounded by massive mountain cliffs with streams pouring off them, Princess Louisa Inlet beckons. Chatterbox Falls at the head of the inlet roars down from a hidden glacier. A world-class yachting destination, "the Princess" attracts boaters of every ilk. Even the most jaded among us is enthralled by the beauty of the inlet. Seven km (4.5 mi) long and less than a mile wide, it feels like the cup of life itself.

Many a colourful character has felt the magical pull of Princess Louisa Inlet. "Mac" Macdonald, an American playboy, fell under its spell, bought the land around Chatterbox Falls

Queens Reach

immediately and spent every summer there for the rest of his life. When he could no longer look after it himself, he donated the land to the people of British Columbia as a park. An international society formed by Macdonald still contributes to the maintenance of the place he so loved.

Thomas Hamilton, an American who made pots of money by inventing the variable pitch propeller, also came under the spell. He built a luxury resort on Malibu Rapids where the inlet begins. Within three years his interest flagged and the place was eventually sold to Young Life, a nondenominational Christian organization, as a summer camp for city kids.

GETTING THERE

Highway 101 meanders through forests and around Sakinaw Lake and Ruby Lake on its way to Earls Cove and the ferry to Powell River. That water you pass is fresh water, home of some favoured local swimming areas. Take your time, as this road is a typical Depression-era construction which wanders all over the landscape.

Watch for the turnoff to Egmont just before you enter the ferry terminal. A right turn and a 6-km (3.6-mi) drive brings you to Egmont. All the paddling trips into Jervis Inlet and the Narrows begin at the government wharf in Egmont.

SUTTON ISLETS– EGMONT PT.– MILLER ISLETS

CAUTIONS

The main hazard in the Skookumchuck Narrows is current. When paddling here it is essential that you have a tide table with you to assess the direction and speed of the current.

Having stated that, we don't wish to imply that you will get sucked into the rapids with the tide. The shallow draft of the kayak allows it to skim the surface with minimal drag from current. The worst problem we've had is getting away from the dock. You hop in your boat, push off and whang—before you get organized you are pasted on the side of a moored boat, held

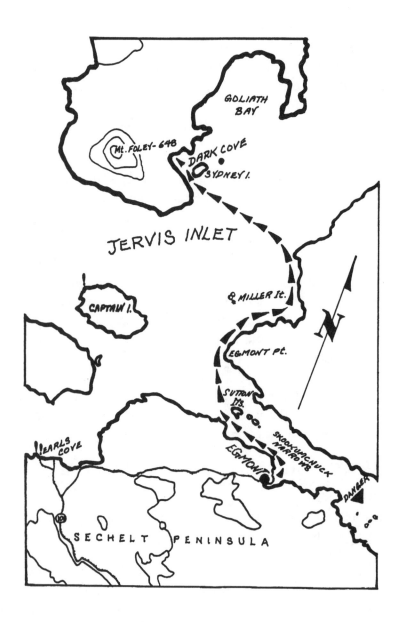

Sutton Islets– Dark Cove

by the force of the current and unable to get your paddle in the water properly. So be sure you are facing into the current when you start.

This is a time to take advantage of the back eddies that swirl through the bays along the shoreline. If the current is against you, keep to the shore to use the back eddy. If it's with you, paddle in the middle.

Need we mention wind again? The area around Egmont is subject to the varying effects of wind and water being pushed through a number of converging channels. Agamemnon Channel, Jervis Inlet both north and west, Skookumchuck Narrows and Hotham Sound all meet here. You will notice eddy lines all over the place and wind changes on short notice.

Jervis Inlet, as mentioned before, is loaded with oysters. We have enjoyed these delectable delights many times. But if you want to try them, check with the Department of Fisheries and Oceans before your trip to be sure that there are no closures due to Red Tide. Shellfish poisoning is fatal. Do not eat oysters unless you are sure they are safe.

There is a lot of boat traffic throughout the region, both recreational and commercial, and all the vessels are bigger than you. Be alert.

THE TRIP

Start from the government wharf at Egmont and paddle west toward the Sutton Islets in the middle of the narrows. We enjoy the old-time flavour of the village with its mix of homes, fish boats and logging equipment, all jumbled together along the shore. Everybody has their own dock and some have added some unusual personal touches.

The tidal flush encourages prolific growth in the sea. Some of the largest anemones we have seen grow off the underside of the wharf in Egmont. At low tide you see those relentless predators, the Sunburst Sea Stars, cruising the seabed like enormous orange space ships. Great Blue Herons and kingfishers hang out in hopes of a meal. Schools of pile perch and other fish congregate under the protection of the floats.

The Sutton Islets are private property and are posted as such. Signs reading Beware of Snakes are further encouragement to stay in your boat. (No snake sightings have ever actually been reported in the area.)

Egmont   Keith Thirkell photo

Supple bull kelp fronds undulate gently over the surface of the water along all sides of these islets. These forests of kelp support a wealth of sea creatures, so watch carefully as you pass by them.

There are caves along the side of the islets where octopus like to hang out, a feature that endears the site to lots of scuba divers. In winter, when visibility in the water can reach 18 to 30 m (60 to 100 feet), you may be able to catch sight of one.

In the old days when boats were the only mode of transportation here, there was more Egmont on the north side of the narrows than on the south side. Nowadays you still see moms taking their kids to school from those homes along that far shore.

At Egmont Point you can see all the various channels that meet in this area. Small wonder that the currents and winds are weird and changeable here. It certainly gives you a chance to practise reading the water surface as you note the various eddy lines and match them to the topography of the area. None of these currents is strong enough to pose a risk to the paddler, so check them out.

North from Egmont Point a couple of rock spires poke out of the water. These are the Miller Islets, looking like a typical seal haulout, and sure enough the sleek, black bodies can be seen lazing at the water's edge when the tide is low. Remember to give them plenty of room.

Marbled Murrelets are common here, as well as all the usual

seabirds of the coast. On one of our trips through the area we saw a pod of orca whales, first in Agamemnon Channel and again the next day by the Miller Islets. A huge male, a couple of smaller females and what seemed to be a youngster made up the group.

When you have seen enough, make your way back to Egmont.

TRIP TIME

At least 3 hours on the water. You'll spent an easy 1 ½ hours of paddling to the Miller Islets, and you should allow extra time if tide and wind are against you.

DARK COVE

CAUTIONS

This trip involves an open water crossing in excess of 3 km (2 mi) to the far shore of Jervis Inlet, increasing the risk from winds. It is well to assess weather conditions carefully before setting out on the crossing.

The beaches throughout Jervis Inlet are covered with oysters below the high-tide line. Although this is not exactly life threatening, it

can play havoc with the finish on your boat and your feet if you don't have proper beach shoes. These shells are razor sharp!

THE TRIP

Launch at Egmont and paddle to the Miller Islets as described in Sutton Islets (above). Continue north across Jervis Inlet toward Sydney Island and the bay behind it, another 2.4 km (1.5 mi) past the islets. There is a small beach at the end of Dark Cove where you can get out of your boat to stretch your legs.

TRIP TIME

A good 6 hours to get there and back. This trip involves almost 16 km (10 mi) of paddling, so take a lunch.

CAPTAIN ISLAND

CAUTIONS

Check that tide table to see what the situation is when you launch from Egmont.

You will cross the area where all those channels converge, giving rise to the possibility of confused wind, waves and cross currents. Expect to see a lot of eddy lines in the water between the head of the Skookumchuck Narrows and Captain Island.

The ferry passes by the island, so keep out of its way. Expect a lot of commercial and recreational boat traffic.

THE TRIP

Launch from Egmont and paddle west, past the Sutton Islets to the mouth of the Skookumchuck Narrows. Captain Island is directly ahead of you just off the point of Nelson Island. If the tide is low, you will find a small beach on the southeast point of the island where you can land. Even at high tide you can get out here, but now you are clambering up onto rocks and logs. Look for a path into the forest above the beach. A short hike into the interior of the island will reveal a few wonderful giants of the forest, old-growth cedar.

Hotham
Sound

TRIP TIME
Plan for 3 hours of paddling, 1 ½ hours each way.

SALTERY BAY TO EGMONT (no map)
Another trip that's fun in Jervis Inlet is to ride the ferry out of
Earls Cove to Saltery Bay and then paddle back. The bonus is
that the ferry trip in that direction is free. There is a public wharf
right beside the Saltery Bay terminal, making the carry to the
launch site reasonably easy. If you have wheels, it's a breeze.

As there is nowhere to get out of the water at Earls Cove,
you will need to leave a vehicle in Egmont and return there.

The prevailing wind in this part of Jervis Inlet blows up the

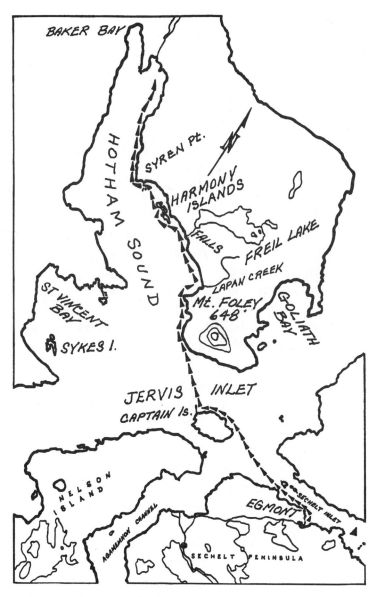

Captain Island– Hotham Sound

inlet, so you are likely to have the wind at your back on this trip. No guarantees, though!

TRIP TIME

5 to 6 hours on the water. This trip is more than 16 km (10 mi).

JERVIS INLET EXTENDED TRIPS

HOTHAM SOUND

CAUTIONS

Check that tide table to see whether the tide is with you or against you on your trip. If you can plan to go with the flow, it will aid you considerably.

This trip involves an open water crossing of 1.6 km (1 mi), so assess the winds before proceeding.

Be aware of the boat traffic when you begin that crossing as there can be a lot of commercial and recreational activity up and down Jervis Inlet.

Hotham Sound is big bear country, so behave accordingly in camp (see pages 34–36). Watch yourself on the oysters that cover the beaches.

THE TRIP

Launch at Egmont, paddle to Captain Island and follow that shore about two-thirds of the way up the island. The idea is to get yourself situated for the shortest jump possible to the opposite shore of the inlet.

Once on the far side, follow the shoreline around into Hotham Sound. The first bay you encounter has a very small beach at the apex which all but disappears with the high tide. On the south side of the bay, find an old log sort where you can camp if necessary. This isn't exactly the most aesthetic site—there is a lot of junk on the shore—but it's good to know about for emergencies.

The best beach in the area is in Granville Bay at the mouth of Lapan Creek. A family lives in a house by the creek, but you can land to stretch your legs if you wish.

As you move up the shore, the roar of Freil Falls beckons you onward. The water drops off the cliff high on the mountainside, appearing and disappearing, dividing and merging as it plummets to the sea below. We have explored the base of the falls on several occasions. The lower areas are pretty easy going, but it quickly becomes apparent that this is not a place for the

Freil Falls

amateur to be fooling around. The rocks are very slippery and
the incline steep! The place is magical, though, both from the
water and along the shore.

Another half mile and you are in the Harmony Islands, a
couple of which are marine park lands. Unfortunately the largest
islands are private land and off limits for campers. The sites are
clearly marked.

On our first trip to the sound, we passed what looked like
a great little beach just before Freil Falls. We thought of camping
there, but kept going. The next day, passing the beach again, we
spotted a dark shape moving around it. As we drifted closer we
could see it was a black bear, turning over rocks and noshing on
the crabs he found there. Boy, were we glad we had given a pass
to that campsite!

If your party is small, we recommend that you camp on
Harmony Island as there are no worries about bears. The

camping areas are small and crowded together but it is a pretty place to stay, with great swimming and a lovely evening lookout. There's also a campsite on the beach behind the most northerly island of the group. A small stream runs past this forest glade with room for a couple of tents. Remember to keep your waste away from the fresh water.

Another couple of miles north of Harmony Island, along the shores of Hotham Sound, you'll find a long, grassy beach with space for a larger party. Check for the high-tide line before you set your camp.

On the opposite shore of the sound, back in the bay behind the prominent orange naval buoys, a local outfitter has established a camp on a logging site. There is a good beach here, lots of room for tents and a makeshift pit toilet. Not a Private Property or No Trespassing sign in sight.

As mentioned earlier, Hotham Sound is an amazingly gentle place in the summer. Even on the hottest days it seems to stay quiet and calm. If you enjoy laid-back days of drifting along on the water, this is the place for you.

CORMORANT

The Pelagic Cormorant is distinguished from the Double-crested Cormorant by its smaller size and the white flashes on the flanks during the breeding season. There are other small differences in the crests and the colours around the beak, but it is difficult to get close enough to these wary birds to see these distinctions.

The Pelagic Cormorant prefers tiny cliff ledges for its skimpy nest of seaweed and feathers, while the Double-crested prefers the clifftop for its more commodious nest of twigs and other debris. Normally silent birds, cormorants will surprise you with the other-worldly groans and hisses they produce during the breeding season.

We saw our first herring boil in Hotham Sound, acres of tiny fish moving in tandem as they darted and rolled. The water beneath us flashed silver as the herring's gleaming undersides caught the light.

If you can time your return trip so you leave the sound on the ebb tide and enter the main inlet and the narrows on the flood tide, you will ease your passage. Summer tides lend themselves to just such planning.

TRIP TIME

At least 3 days is recommended. It takes 3 hours to paddle to the Harmony Islands in good conditions, and if you need to move on to the next campsite, add 1 hour. This means 1 day to get to camp and 1 day to get home again. We have done this trip in 2 days but didn't get much chance to relax and explore the area.

VANCOUVER BAY

CAUTIONS

Wind, wind and more wind is the story in Jervis Inlet. The configuration of the inlet makes it a classic spot for those daily

Vancouver Bay

winds that rise in the morning and subside in late afternoon. In the absence of long fetches the waves can't get that big, but when the energy of the opposing tide is  added in, you find some pretty respectable 2- to 3-foot seas. Talk about your local weather! We have turned a corner into another reach and gone from flat water to 2-foot chop in minutes.

Only occasionally does a bay with a beach intrude on the sheer walls of the inlet, leaving the hapless boater with no refuge along most of its length. This calls for good planning, travelling in the early morning and evening and picking your haulouts carefully according to your skills.

The weather in winter is truly ghastly, cold and very windy. The Jervis Express, an outflow wind similar to the Squamish of Howe Sound, can reach awesome proportions. This is probably a good place to avoid in winter but a pure delight in summer.

Logging companies are active along Jervis Inlet. Expect to see some clearcuts on the slopes and helicopter bases on barges at the shoreline.

THE TRIP
Launch from Egmont and head out past the Sutton Islets and around Egmont Point. Paddle north along the shoreline. Your route will take you along the base of steep bluffs with the occasional rock outcrop and shallow bay. In spring there will be lots of streams flowing off the mountains, in summer many of them will be dry.

Try to take advantage of the tidal flow to help you on your way. Paddle in the centre when going with the flow and along the edge to catch the back eddies if the tide is against you.

The wide bowl of Vancouver Bay opens to the north just after you make the turn into Prince of Wales Reach. A broad, thickly forested valley carries the Vancouver River down to the head of the bay, creating a long mud flat topped with a narrow grassy beach.

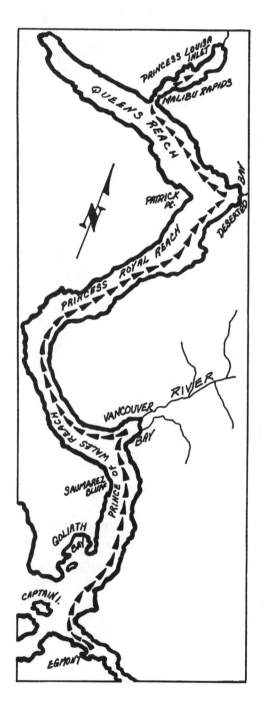

Vancouver Bay–
Princess Louisa Inlet

All the land around the bay is either reserve land or leased to the Sechelt Band by the forest company that owns the property. The reserve is a small snippet of land to the left of the river mouth. Several abandoned buildings are being swallowed up by the forest along the shore. There are good camping sites here and on the right bank of the river. The band allows people to use this area freely if they check in at the band office in Sechelt before the trip.

On the other side of the head of the bay you will see a number of buildings and a small dock. This is the site of a treatment centre for native youth. Visitors are requested to stay away from this area.

There is a nice trail up the Vancouver River through some beautiful patches of woods, in a splendid example of temperate rain forest. We were fortunate to see an American Dipper on this river. This unique bird looks like a large, grey wren but it actually dives and swims beneath the swift waters to walk along the streambed gathering food.

TRIP TIME
2 full days to get there and back. It is a 19-km (12-mi) paddle to Vancouver Bay. We do not recommend this trip unless you are an experienced paddler with a reasonable level of fitness.

PRINCESS LOUISA INLET

CAUTIONS
The hazards previously outlined are the same for this trip over many more miles of water.

Malibu Rapids at the opening of Princess Louisa runs up to

*In nature's book of secrecy
A little I can read.*
—Shakespeare

10 knots with a big flood tide. You will need to run the rapids with a flood tide or you won't get into the inlet. If the range of the tide is wide you should wait till close to slack before attempting the rapids.

THE TRIP

The first leg of your trip will put you in Vancouver Bay as outlined in the Vancouver Bay trip (above).

The next stretch covers the rest of Prince of Wales Reach and Princess Royal Reach to Deserted Bay, another very long paddle. Mountain peaks soar up on every side, many of them covered with snow through most of the year. We have seen mountain goats on these steep crags, but you need binoculars to pick them out.

Native reserve land runs from the mouth of Stakawus Creek about 1.6 km (1 mi) south of the bay to the north side of Deserted Bay. The creek marks the beginning of a long stretch of gently sloped land that offers good camping opportunities. Watch those oysters when you land.

The final leg of the trip takes you to the campground behind Macdonald Island in the Inlet. We prefer this campground to the one farther up the inlet at Chatterbox Falls, as it is quieter and drier.

As you paddle along the north side of Queens Reach, watch for Malibu Camp and the rapids beside it. In spite of having been there many times, we still find it creeps up on us unexpectedly. Suddenly we're right on top of it. Built from local logs, the lodge has a natural grey patina that blends perfectly into the background. This fascinating array of rustic buildings is graced with totem poles generously sprinkled about the grounds. Although the Sechelts did not traditionally erect totem poles, they certainly used wood carvings on their buildings. These poles are fine examples of the skill of the local craftsmen.

As you have timed your trip to arrive here on a flood tide, you can run the rapids into the inlet. At full flood on a big tide

Princess Louisa Inlet

there will be a .3-m (1-foot) overfall at the point and about 300 m (1000 feet) of turbulence and whirlpools on the inside. There are no rocks in the path of the rapids to cause you grief, just a good volume of water running fast. If you feel comfortable with this kind of water condition, it is lots of fun to play in these rapids. Come back with an empty boat to really enjoy the experience.

Once inside, you are looking at one of British Columbia's natural jewels. Steep cliffs soar to the sky on every side with freshets of water pouring off them. Some dance down the precipice with great displays of spray and spume while others slide quietly along the surface.

The Princess is just 7 km (4.5 mi) long, less than 600 m (1 mi) wide and very deep. In summer the wall of mountains protects it from wind so the water is almost always calm and flat. In winter, outflows can be harsh.

The public campground sits on the point behind Macdonald Island with the buildings of the Young Life hiking camp to the left of it. In the off season, you are invited to use these buildings if necessary. We have taken them up on this offer on occasion

Malibu Rapids

when it has been pouring rain during our visit, and it's been a real bonus.

From this base camp it is a 20-minute paddle to the head of the inlet. About halfway there you will pass Echo Rock, a sheer rock face that bounces sound back and forth across the inlet several times on good days. If the tide is low, look at the bottom of the intertidal zone for hordes of tubeworms waving their tiny pink tentacles in the current. We once saw a translucent little nudibranch waving in the water along this cliff.

Chatterbox Falls, mother of all the falls in the inlet, thunders down to the water surface at the apex of the inlet. A huge bowl rests above the falls, collecting water from the glacier hidden in the mountains. From the other side of the inlet you see the stream growing as it winds through this bowl on its way to the sea.

Yes, Chatterbox Falls is everything that everyone has claimed. In the actual experience, its beauty is indescribable. Standing at the foot of this display, one feels to be at the very source of life itself, in a sacred spot triggering peace and spiritual renewal. On either side the mountains are high and rugged, showing the scars formed when the moving glaciers cut their way through.

We paddle right up to where the creek water joins with the ocean. Churned up by the plunging waters, swirls of bubbling froth are drawn and redrawn over the sea surface where creek and sea meet. Trees and rocks are draped in heavy green moss. Once on shore we step with caution, as the ground and rocks feel greased and dangerously slippery. It is impossible to carry on a conversation beneath the falls. The roaring, throbbing waters of Chatterbox overwhelm our senses. Large veils of mist drift far out into the inlet, at times all but blanking out the far bank.

On one visit in the late fall, the water around the falls was teeming with huge pink jellyfish wafting gently along, tentacles trailing—delicate parachutists of the sea. When they are in season it is best to swim elsewhere as the long tentacles carry a nasty sting.

On the return trip you will want to catch an ebb tide out of the inlet and use these tides as much as possible to help you home. You are more likely to be paddling into the wind on this journey so plan accordingly.

TRIP TIME

At least 2 days to get to and from the inlet, and this is cutting it short indeed. 3 days each way is preferred. Add a couple of days at least to enjoy the full flavour of this magical place.

Lund

The northern end of the Sunshine Coast is bounded by Desolation Sound, another mountain-ringed island-clogged expanse of sea reaching into the valleys of mainland British Columbia. It is here that the tidal currents meet after making their way around both ends of Vancouver Island. This means the tidal exchange is minimal throughout the area, resulting in generally warmer water. Not only humans but oysters delight in this happy circumstance. The shores of Desolation Sound support masses of these delectable little critters.

Like the broom that blooms each spring all up and down the coast, these oysters are an introduced species. The native oysters are much smaller and have been virtually wiped out by the interlopers. In the early 1900s, some enterprising individual decided that the bigger, faster-growing Japanese oyster was more economically viable so he planted a few in Pender Harbour. From that modest foothold they have exuberantly colonized the whole coast.

The landscape between Jervis Inlet and Desolation Sound is dotted with basins of fresh water. Powell Lake rivals the Sechelt Inlet in size, stretching deep into the mountain valleys behind the town interconnecting with many smaller lakes and rivers. The rivers and falls that once carried these waters to the sea have been diverted or destroyed in the service of the forest industry, but the lakes continue to be favourite haunts for boaters.

Desolation Sound   Keith Thirkell photo

The town of Powell River is the largest settlement along the Sunshine Coast. Life here is dominated by a single feature, the pulp and paper mill sitting at the ocean's edge at the north end of town. Built in the early 1900s, it once supported the company town that marches up the slopes beside the mill. The old townsite is now a heritage site as it so perfectly preserves the ambience of that era.

Forests in the area were logged in the early part of the century, and the Powell River area is now home to a vigorous second-growth forest offering a host of recreational values for the hiker, boater and camper.

Some 48 km (30 mi) past Powell River is Lund, the end of the road, the final stop on Highway 101 (or the start of it, depending on your point of view), the Pan American highway whose other end begins in Terra del Fuego, Chile. Lund is another picturesque coastal village, clustered around the Malaspina Hotel. This splendid old heritage building was constructed early in the century and continues to serve the community and visitors admirably with a pub, restaurant, general store, parking, rooms to rent, water taxi and marina.

The Malaspina Inlet and Okeover Inlet spread down from Desolation Sound to carve out Malaspina Peninsula. The islands that clog the channel at the top of Vancouver Island start here with Savary Island, then Hernando, then Cortes and on up to Johnstone Strait.

GETTING THERE

The ferry from Earls Cove heads through Jervis Inlet to Saltery Bay, where you pick up Highway 101 again. On leaving the ferry terminal, drive over a high ridge before dropping down to the gentle slopes of the seashore.

Continue through Powell River, past the mill and out the other side of town. It is about 48 km (30 mi) to Lund at the end of the road. There is lots of parking in the lot around the hotel. Please note it is paid parking.

The turnoff for the Okeover Inlet, Galley Bay Road, is clearly indicated by signs about 5 km (3 mi) before Lund. There is a provincial park at the end of this road, with plenty of parking.

SAVARY ISLAND

Savary Island arcs gracefully off the coast about a mile from Lund. Another of those enormous sand dunes thrown up by mysterious forces of the sea, Savary is known locally as the Hawaii of BC. Long beaches of white sand slide gently into the shallow, sun-warmed sea, supporting all kinds of flora and

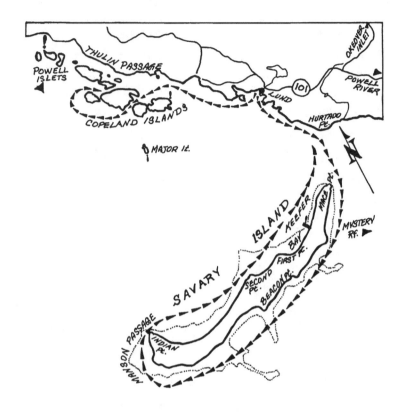

Copeland Islands–Savary Island

fauna. At low tide the combination of rock, seaweed and sand brings to mind a Japanese water garden.

It is here that the tidal currents from the north and south meet as they sweep around Vancouver Island. The minimal tidal exchange creates particularly warm water all through this area, a real boon for the swimmer as the water is warmer here than anywhere else on the coast.

Savary's unique features do not end there. While all the other islands along the coast line up parallel to the mainland, Savary curves out almost at a right angle to the shore. Towering banks of sand in distinct stratas face south, while the north side of the island slopes softly into the water.

Peeps race along the water's edge foraging through the fine

Savary Island

sand, while seals roll and dive in the shallows pursuing the small fish that proliferate here.

The world's largest arbutus tree twists out of the side of a sandy bank just up the road from the government wharf on the north side of the island. This road mounts the spine of the island and then meanders over its length.

GETTING THERE

Launch from the government wharf in Lund and paddle across to the island. The wharf on Savary is about a third of the way up the north side of the island.

The water taxi from Lund will take you and your kayaks over to the island for a small fee if you prefer to avoid the crossing.

CAUTIONS

Wind from the south and the west will affect the paddler on the crossing to the island. Funnelling and channelling effects will augment the waves at the headlands, especially at the east end of the island. The high cliffs around the east end deflect the waves, creating confused seas with standing waves. Waves start to steepen and break when they "feel" the bottom, so you may find that relatively gentle swells turn into breakers over the long flats that extend from the south side of the island.

One side of the island or the other will be the lee side, so once you have made the crossing you can find a haven. The view from Lund can be deceiving—the island looks so close and the harbour so protected—but don't be taken in. The wildest ride we have ever had in a kayak was on this crossing.

Lots of boat traffic comes and goes from Lund, so be alert. Remember, turn to starboard (right) to avoid collision.

There is no water on Savary so be sure to bring enough for your stay.

THE TRIP

The approach to the island depends on the wind direction when you launch. We prefer the south face of the island as the dwellings are all up on the high bank, leaving the beach relatively untouched. If the weather permits, head for Mace Point, the eastern headland, and follow the south shore. What a pleasure to pull up on a smooth sand beach with no worries about rocks or barnacles or oysters to mar your hull or cut your

Savary Island

feet. These are ideal waters to play in. Try your Eskimo roll or practice those braces. The water is like warm soup on sunny summer days.

This is also a particularly fine place for a bit of snorkelling. The many kelp beds and patches of rocks through the shallows provide cover for a variety of sea life. The flats reach almost 5 km (3 mi) out into the ocean from the southeast face of the island, giving you a lot of area to explore. Look for the buoy that marks Mystery Reef at the limit of the shallows.

The circumnavigation of the island is an easy paddle, so spend some quality time on those lovely beaches. You can walk across the island along the road in an hour or so if you enjoy the change of pace. Return to Lund in the quiet of the evening.

If you want to camp, remember that the beach will be covered entirely in a really high tide, so make sure you are above the high-tide line. There are no designated campgrounds on the island but we have seen campers snuggled up in the bushes on low-lying land along the shore. We have stayed in a bed-and-breakfast, leaving our kayaks at the base of the cliff. This is a pretty deluxe way to enjoy the island.

TRIP TIME

1 day. The crossing to the island takes about 30 minutes and the circumnavigation is about 3 hours, so take a full day to enjoy Savary Island.

THE COPELAND ISLANDS

About a mile and a half northwest of Lund sit the Copeland Islands, a string of rocky outcrops separated from the coast by the very narrow Thulin Passage. These are your typical storm-tossed rocks with fringes of gnarled pine and fir trees clinging stubbornly to the highest points. The whole archipelago is designated the Copeland Islands Marine Park.

Lund

GETTING THERE
Launch from the government wharf in Lund and paddle north-west along the shoreline to the islands (see Savary Island map).

CAUTIONS
Wind is the major hazard facing the paddler here. Thulin Passage between the islands and the mainland is very narrow and the mainland shore is high cliffs, the ideal configuration to funnel and strengthen the wind. It can be a lot of work to paddle against the wind to or from the Copelands.

THE TRIP
Once out of the bay at Lund, you leave behind most of the human settlement, although there is some development along here. The islands lie low in the water with edges that drop off abruptly into deep water. It is interesting to poke around the wrinkled shore to see what lives down there. The shoreline teems with sea stars of every type grazing the rich oyster beds. At the lowest level of the intertidal zone, look for sea cucumbers, tubeworms and sea urchins.

In spring the islands will sport a variety of wildflowers

common all along the coast. Wild sedums of many types love these hot, dry environments.

Look for Common Mergansers poking about in the little passages between the islands and Black Oystercatchers foraging in the intertidal zone. Orca whales are a fairly common sight through this area, so keep a weather eye out. You might get lucky!

Camping is permitted on all the islands and it is easy to find reasonable spots for 3 or 4 tents. As the soil cover is minimal, it is probably best to use the sea for human waste if you cannot carry it out with you.

If you choose to stay on the island, take a trip out to the Powell Islets to the northwest and Major Islet to the south to see what's up out there.

TRIP TIME

About 30 minutes in good conditions. This is a good choice for an afternoon of paddling.

Okeover Inlet–
Desolation Sound

OKEOVER INLET

A Y-shaped system of inlets forms the northeast side of Malaspina Peninsula. The foot of the Y is Okeover Inlet with Lancelot Inlet and Malaspina Inlet as the two arms.

This body of water is a protected and gentle place to explore by kayak. The mountainous edges are thickly forested with lots of homes and cottages lining the shore. Many of the beaches have shellfish operations on them, so obey the signs to keep off!

The northern extremity of Lancelot Inlet is within a hundred feet or so of Portage Cove on Desolation Sound. Do not be tempted to try the portage. That little piece of land is privately owned, although it is in the middle of Desolation Sound Marine Park, and trespassing is strictly prohibited.

The area is dotted with islets of various sizes and bays of

various depths, offering plenty of features to explore. Oysters proliferate throughout this area as they love the warm, quiet water here. This encourages predators, most notably the sea stars that ooze through shellfish colonies, gorging themselves.

Expect to see all the usual seabirds that frequent the coast. Kingfishers, Great Blue Herons, eagles, mergansers, Marbled Murrelets and oystercatchers thrive in these rich waters.

CAUTIONS

This is a particularly good spot for novices, or anyone who prefers a quieter trip. The twists and turns of the inlets, the many islets and bays offer refuge from the daily winds, and there is no need to cross open water anywhere.

The prolific growth of oysters may tempt you to try one. Check with the Department of Fisheries and Oceans for Red Tide information. And don't take more than the limit.

GETTING THERE

Highway 101 leaves Powell River north of town, climbs a ridge along the side of Powell Lake and heads northwest along the Malaspina Peninsula.

Watch the right-hand side of the road about 40 km (25 mi) from Powell River for signs indicating Okeover Inlet Provincial Park. Once you catch sight of the water, keep to the left until you enter the parking lot of the park at the water's edge. If you want to camp in the park, drive through the parking lot and into the campsite area.

THE TRIP

Once you have launched into Okeover Inlet, there are several spots you can head for depending on the time available to you. One of our favourites is to paddle up the west side of Okeover and follow along Coode Peninsula and Coode Island. The tidal current rushes through the little pass between the peninsula and the island into Trevenen Bay, exposing the marine creatures to our scrutiny.

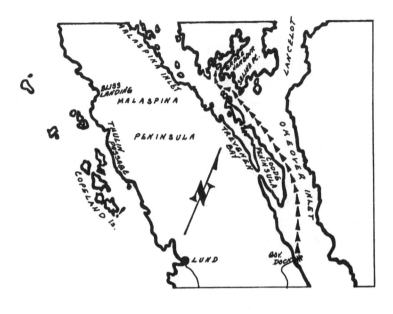

Okeover Inlet

Where the tidal flow is squeezed between Coode Island and Selina Point on Gifford Peninsula, the current reaches about 2 knots, enough to increase the work of paddling a bit. This is the start of Malaspina Inlet.

Grace Harbour, a long, narrow bay, pushes into the coast of the Gifford Peninsula just beyond this point. A short stretch of land along the north side of the harbour opposite the island at the mouth of the bay is Native reserve land. There is a campground at the end of the bay and lots of opportunities to land along the south side. On every trip we have taken to this area, we have stopped for lunch in Grace Harbour.

A short walk inland from the north side of the head of the harbour brings you to a small marsh and lake filled with lily pads and sunken logs, a peaceful spot for some rest and relaxation.

You can spend as much time as you like exploring the rest

of these inlets. Lancelot Inlet has a lot of nooks and crannies to drift around as you enjoy the luxurious marine garden. The shoreline carries many relics of the past—overgrown orchards, crumbling settlements and rusting tools.

Theodosia Inlet opens through a narrow pass off the north side of Lancelot Inlet. Expect a bit of current through here, but it will be quite gentle. There is a large Native reserve at the end of the inlet with a vast mud flat in front of it that dries at low tide. Be careful you don't get grounded in here. The tide retreats at an amazing rate over shallows like these and slogging through mud pulling a kayak is no fun at all. Yes, we are speaking from experience!

TRIP TIME

3 to 4 hours paddling to Grace Harbour and back. But you can spend an afternoon or several days just cruising around these inlets. If you like laid-back paddling in a protected environment with lots of little nooks and crannies to poke about in, this is the spot for you.

DESOLATION SOUND EXTENDED TRIPS

Desolation Sound Provincial Marine Park is the largest park in the region. It encompasses the whole of Malaspina Inlet and Gifford Peninsula, the northern end of Lancelot Inlet, and the shore of Desolation Sound to a mile or so past Prideaux Haven. Legislation is pending to designate the Curmes Islets, off the northern end of Mink Island, part of the park as well. While the government has purchased the majority of the land in this area, there are a few exceptions. The most notable is the narrow strip connecting the top of Lancelot Inlet to Portage Bay in Desolation Sound. This is private property and not available to the public,

Desolation Sound

tempting as it is! There is also a row of summer cottages on the shore just south of Grace Harbour.

This sound is another popular yachting destination, so expect to see a lot of boat traffic in the summer months. Fortunately they tend to congregate in the best moorages, like Prideaux Haven, leaving lots of room for the kayaker to find solitude.

There are few beaches around the sound, making it more difficult to find camping spots, especially for large parties. You'll have no trouble setting up 1 or 2 kayaks on a little islet or a rock shelf.

CAUTIONS

If you stick to the park you will be doing primarily shoreline paddling in an enclosed environment, keeping the risks to a minimum. The long, narrow inlets off the sound are subject to the daily winds.

If you decide to cross to the Redonda Islands or Cortes Island, you will be exposed to the winds of the Strait of Georgia coming up the full fetch of the strait. So assess your situation carefully before poking your nose past the lee of Malaspina Peninsula. We took one memorable trip along the west side of the Peninsula to the Copeland Islands in the teeth of a fierce gale and pelting rain. The beaches are few and far between on this stretch and we found refuge only after a couple of hours of tough paddling.

If you venture into the passes between the many islands between the mainland and Vancouver Island, be aware that there are some fierce rapids that are only navigable at slack tide. Do not travel here without a chart, a tide table and some good local knowledge.

If you have more than one vehicle available, you may wish to park one in Lund and the other on Okeover Inlet. Now you have a choice of landing spots on your return.

Desolation Sound

THE TRIP

Launch into Okeover Inlet and paddle up to Malaspina Inlet. Grace Harbour makes a good rest spot before heading out into Desolation Sound. Malaspina Inlet is filled with little islets and bays, giving you a huge marine garden to explore.

Follow the western shore around Zephine Head into Galley Bay. There are a number of little islets in the north corner of the bay that make a pleasant campsite for the night. We spent a memorable night cooking oysters over a little fire and watching the moon rise over the sound. A touch of wine, a bit of cheese and a sprinkling of wild chive on oysters cooked on a wood fire—sheer ambrosia, we can tell you!

Spend some time exploring the shoreline. Tenedos Bay, Otter Island and all the islands around Prideaux Haven will keep you enthralled for the whole day. We met a school of herring here, amazing numbers of lovely silver fish packed into small bays along the shore.

Marbled Murrelets enjoy these waters, so keep an eye open for these compact little diving birds. Common Loons are everywhere in the spring. We once saw a mother loon cruising quietly along with her brood of chicks riding on her low-slung back.

The Curme Islands off the northern tip of Mink Island offer deluxe campsites for small parties. Camping on little islets like these ensures peaceful nights free of critters.

On the third day our plan was to paddle to Squirrel Cove on Cortes Island after poking around the Martin Islands (just off the southern tip of West Redonda Island), Refuge Cove (on West Redonda Island), and Kinghorn Island (midway between Cortes, Redonda and the top end of Malaspina Peninsula). We still think this is an excellent plan, if the weather cooperates.

Refuge Cove is a lovely, protected spot with a small settlement. A restaurant that only operates in the summer months serves cinnamon buns to die for—a good lunch stop.

Squirrel Cove on Cortes Island is a Native reserve with colourful houses and a neat general store with goods both ordinary and unusual. There is a campground back in the cove for public use.

We spent the final day of our trip here returning to Lund with a stopoff on the Copelands. We had the option of paddling down Okeover Inlet if the weather was the pits, as we had vehicles in both places.

TRIP TIME

4 days, with at least 4 hours of paddling every day. When we did this trip, we were on the water for even longer than that, as we did a lot of poking around.

OTHER EXTENDED TRIPS

There are a wealth of places to go in the Desolation Sound area. Consider jumping from Savary to Hernando to Cortes to Redonda Islands and back. Teakerne Arm on Redonda Island is another favourite destination. The possibilities are endless.

Further Reading

Burch, David. 1993. *Fundamentals of Kayak Navigation*, 2nd ed. Old Saybrook CT: Globe Pequot Press.

Dowd, John. 1988. *Sea Kayaking: A Manual for Long Distance Touring*, 3rd paper ed. Vancouver: Douglas & McIntyre Ltd.

Environment Canada. 1993. *Marine Weather Hazards Manual: A Guide to Local Forecasts and Conditions*, 2nd ed. Vancouver: Gordon Soules.

Guignet, Charles Joseph. n.d. *The Birds of British Columbia*. Handbook #6 and #8. Victoria: Royal BC Museum (BC Provincial Museum).

Hutchinson, Derek C. 1990. *Derek C. Hutchinson's Guide to Sea Kayaking*, 2nd ed. Old Saybrook CT: Globe Pequot Press.

Lee, Albert. 1976. *Weather Wisdom*. Garden City NY: Doubleday.

Peterson, Roger Tory. 1990. *A Field Guide to Western Birds*, 3rd ed. NY: Houghton Mifflin.

Russo, Ron and Olhausen, Pam. 1981. *Pacific Intertidal Life*. Berkeley CA: Nature Study Guild.

White, Howard. 1990. *Writing in the Rain*. Madeira Park BC: Harbour Publishing.

White, Howard. 1996. *The Sunshine Coast*. Madeira Park BC: Harbour Publishing.

Wolferstan, Bill. 1982. *Pacific Yachting's Cruising Guide to British Columbia, vol. 3*. Vancouver: McLean Hunter Ltd.

Udvardy, Miklos D.F. 1988. *The Audubon Society Field Guide to North American Birds, Western Region*. Toronto: Random House.

Index